GHO_._

Henrik Ibsen

GHOSTS

A Domestic Tragedy in Three Acts

translated by Stephen Unwin

OBERON BOOKS
LONDON

WWW.OBERONBOOKS.COM

First published in 2013 by Oberon Books Ltd
521 Caledonian Road, London N7 9RH
Tel: +44 (0) 20 7607 3637 / Fax: +44 (0) 20 7607 3629
e-mail: info@oberonbooks.com
www.oberonbooks.com

A catalogue record for this book is available from the British
Library.

PB ISBN: 978-1-78319-052-2
E ISBN: 978-1-78319-551-0

Cover design by feastcreative.com

Visit www.oberonbooks.com to read more about all our books
and to buy them. You will also find features, author interviews and
news of any author events, and you can sign up for e-newsletters
so that you're always first to hear about our new releases.

This production of *Ghosts* was first produced by Rose Theatre
Kingston and English Touring Theatre on 19 September 2013
at the Rose Theatre Kingston.

ENGSTRAND	Pip Donaghy
PASTOR MANDERS	Patrick Drury
REGINA ENGSTRAND	Florence Hall
MRS ALVING	Kelly Hunter
OSVALD ALVING	Mark Quartley

Director	Stephen Unwin
Designer	Simon Higlett
Lighting Designer	Paul Pyant
Composer	Corin Buckeridge
Dramaturg	Sue Prideaux
Casting Director	Ginny Schiller CDG
Assistant Director	Kim Pearce

English Touring Theatre is one of the UK's most successful and exciting production companies, widely regarded as England's National Theatre of Touring.

Led by Director Rachel Tackley, the company works with leading artists to stage an eclectic mix of new and classic work for audiences throughout the UK and overseas; theatre that is thrilling, popular and, above all, entertaining.

ETERNAL LOVE
THE STORY OF ABELARD & HELOISE
Spring 2014

GHOSTS
Autumn 2013

THE MISANTHROPE
Spring 2013

THURSDAY
Spring 2013

THE SACRED FLAME
Autumn 2012

THE REAL THING
Summer 2012

*"English, touring and theatre are three wonderful words.
Put together they are more wonderful still"*

- Sir Ian McKellen, Patron

ARTS COUNCIL
ENGLAND
Supported using public funding by
LOTTERY FUNDED

ett.org.uk

@ETTtweet
/EnglishTouringTheatre

ROSE THEATRE KINGSTON

Nestled on the banks of the River Thames in the heart of Kingston, the Rose Theatre is a cultural centre for people from across South West London and beyond.

Since opening in 2008, the Rose has grown to be a powerhouse of producing theatre, mounting over 20 productions in its first five years.

Ghosts is Stephen Unwin's fourteenth production for the Rose, and marks his swansong as Artistic Director.

A DAY IN THE DEATH OF JOE EGG

★★★★
The Daily Mail

THE VORTEX

★★★★★
The Daily Telegraph

THE LADY FROM THE SEA

★★★★
The Independent, The Times

THE IMPORTANCE OF BEING EARNEST

★★★★
The Sunday Times, The Independent

HAY FEVER

★★★★
The Evening Standard, The Daily Telegraph

THE WINSLOW BOY

★★★★★
The Daily Mail

'Stephen Unwin is the finest director of Ibsen in Britain' The Guardian

rosetheatrekingston.org

A note on the translation

*In respect of language, Ibsen stands at a unique disadvantage. Never
before has a poet of world wide fame appealed to his world wide
audience so exclusively in translations.*
William Archer

Ibsen knew that he wrote in a 'small language' and that if his plays
were to have an impact, they would have to be translated.

Ibsen's Norwegian is remarkably spare and direct. Indeed, some
early critics dismissed his naturalistic plays as having little literary
value. But that is to misunderstand Ibsen's intentions, as he wrote in
a letter of 1883:

*In the last seven or eight years, I have hardly written a single line of
verse; instead I have exclusively studied the incomparably more difficult
art of writing in the straightforward honest language of reality.*

Furthermore, Ibsen specified that his plays should be translated into
the everyday language of the audience to whom they are played. My
aim has been to give the actors space and not load them down with
too many words.

But Ibsen was a great poet and very particular in his intentions.
I've resisted the temptation to use English's huge vocabulary to soften
the pattern of repeated words that creates the text's allusive character,
and I've tried to ensure that the more poetic phrases arise from the
character's responses to the situation and don't feel imposed. I've
avoided English Victorianisms or additional explanatory phrases.
I've also tried to retain a sense of nineteenth-century social *mores* and
convey something of the play's particular Scandinavian atmosphere.

Like many translators of Ibsen, I'm dependent on others. I've
drawn on several translations, especially early ones, and Sue Prideaux
has helped me with dozens of details. And then, of course, there are
the actors: in just a few short days of rehearsal they helped me improve
it enormously. To all, our thanks.

Translation is always and inevitably a compromise. I hope I've
created something which the actors will enjoy playing and the
audiences will want to engage with. Ibsen's great play deserves no less.

Stephen Unwin

Characters

MRS ALVING

OSWALD ALVING, her son

PASTOR MANDERS

ENGSTRAND, a carpenter

REGINA ENGSTRAND, in Mrs Alving's service

The action takes place at Mrs Alving's house
on one of the larger fjords of Western Norway.

ACT ONE

A large garden-room with a door on the left, and two on the right. In the middle, a round table with chairs, books, magazines and newspapers. In the land on the left, a window, with a small sofa and a sewing table. At the back, a conservatory smaller than the room, with large glass walls. On the right wall of the conservatory, a door leads into the garden. Through the windows, a gloomy fjord landscape can be seen, half-hidden by pouring rain.

ENGSTRAND is by the garden door. His left leg is slightly deformed, and he wears a boot with a clump of wood under the sole. REGINA, with an empty garden syringe in her hand, is trying to stop him coming in.

REGINA: *(Under her breath.)* What do you want? Stay where you are. You're soaking wet.

ENGSTRAND: It's God's own rain, my girl.

REGINA: The Devil's own rain, more like it.

ENGSTRAND: Good Lord, the way you talk, Regina.

Takes a few limping steps forward.

But what I wanted to say was this –

REGINA: Don't clump around like that. The young master's asleep, upstairs.

ENGSTRAND: At midday?

REGINA: It's no business of yours.

ENGSTRAND: I was out on a spree last night –

REGINA: I'm sure.

ENGSTRAND: Aye, well, we're all mortal flesh, my girl –

REGINA: Aren't we just?

ENGSTRAND: – and legion are the temptations of this world – but, as God is my witness, I was hard at work at half five this morning.

REGINA: I'm sure, but now clear off, will you? I'm not standing around as if I had a rendezvous with you.

ENGSTRAND: A what?

REGINA: I don't want anyone to find you here. So now you know, beat it.

ENGSTRAND: *(Coming a few steps nearer.)* Not a chance. Not till we've had a wee chat. I'll have finished work on the schoolhouse this afternoon, and I'll be on the steamer back to town tonight.

REGINA: *(Mutters.)* Have a nice trip.

ENGSTRAND: Thanks, my girl. Tomorrow's the opening of the orphanage, and there's bound to be a right old knees up and plenty of drink. And I don't want anyone saying that Jacob Engstrand gives in to temptation.

REGINA: No.

ENGSTRAND: There'll be plenty of fine folk here. And Pastor Manders is expected from town.

REGINA: He's coming today.

ENGSTRAND: There you are, you see. And I won't have him saying anything against me.

REGINA: Oh, so that's your game, is it?

ENGSTRAND: What do you mean?

REGINA: *(Suspiciously.)* What are you going to trick the Pastor out of this time?

ENGSTRAND: Are you mad? Why would I want to trick Pastor Manders? No, no – he's much too good a friend for that. But what I wanted to talk to you about, see, was my going back home tonight.

REGINA: The sooner the better, if you ask me.

ENGSTRAND: Aye, but I want you to come with me, Regina.

REGINA: *(Astonished.)* You want what?

ENGSTRAND: I want to take you home.

REGINA: *(Contemptuously.)* I'm not going home with you.

ENGSTRAND: We'll see about that.

REGINA: Yes, we will. Mrs Alving has brought me up like a lady – as one of her own – d'you think I'd go home with *you*? – to a house like that? No chance.

ENGSTRAND: What the hell do you mean? Are you setting yourself up against your own father, you little hussy?

REGINA: *(Mutters, without looking at him.)* You've often said you had nothing to do with me.

ENGSTRAND: Pah – why do you listen to that?

REGINA: The number of times you've called me a b – ? For shame.

ENGSTRAND: I never used that word.

REGINA: I know what you called me.

ENGSTRAND: Anyway, that was when I was a bit, well... You know. Many are the temptations of this world, Regina.

REGINA: Oh, God.

ENGSTRAND: Or when your mother was in a temper. I had to find some way of getting back at her, my girl. Always so la-di-da.

Mimicking her.

'Let me go, Engstrand, let me go. I worked for the Alvings at Rosenvold for three years when he was Court Chamberlain.'

Laughs.

Oh yes, she never forgot that Captain Alving was ennobled when she was in service here.

REGINA: Poor mother – you worried her into her grave.

ENGSTRAND: *(Shrugging his shoulders.)* Oh, aye, I'm to blame for everything.

REGINA: *(Beneath her breath, as she turns away.)* And that leg.

ENGSTRAND: What did you say, my girl?

REGINA: Pied de mouton.

ENGSTRAND: Is that French?

REGINA: Yes.

ENGSTRAND: Well, you've certainly got yourself an education out here, no mistake. It might come in handy one day, Regina.

REGINA: *(After a short silence.)* So why do you want me back in town?

ENGSTRAND: Need you ask why a father wants his only child? Aren't I a poor and lonely widower?

REGINA: Oh, don't give me that. What do you want me to do?

ENGSTRAND: Well, you see, I'm thinking of starting a new line of work.

REGINA: *(Whistles.)* You've tried that before – it always ends in tears.

ENGSTRAND: But this time you'll see, Regina. I'll bloody well –

REGINA: *(Stamping her foot.)* Please stop swearing.

ENGSTRAND: Quite right, my girl, quite right. I just wanted to say that I've put a few pennies aside from working up here on the new orphanage.

REGINA: Really? Good for you.

ENGSTRAND: What's a man to spend his money on out here?

REGINA: And?

ENGSTRAND: Well, you see, I thought of putting the money into something that would pay. A home for sailors –

REGINA: Urgh.

ENGSTRAND: A classy place, of course – not a pigsty. Damn it, no, for captains and first mates. Classy folk, you know.

REGINA: And what would I do?

ENGSTRAND: Help out. Just for show. Wouldn't be hard work, I promise. You'd do what you like.

REGINA: I see.

ENGSTRAND: We'd have to have ladies around, obviously. Because in the evening we want to make the place nice – singing, dancing, that sort of thing. They're sailors, Regina – travellers on the oceans of life.

Coming nearer to her.

So don't be a fool and stand in the way. What are you going to do out here? This education of yours, what's the use of that? You're going to look after the wee ones in the orphanage: is that what you want? D'you want to chuck away your youth for the sake of those dirty brats?

REGINA: Not if things work out the way I want them to – Well, they might, who knows? They might.

ENGSTRAND: What might?

REGINA: Never you mind. So, have you put a lot of money by then, out here?

ENGSTRAND: Seven or eight hundred kroner.

REGINA: Not bad.

ENGSTRAND: Enough to get me started, my girl.

REGINA: Aren't you going to give any of it to me?

ENGSTRAND: Of course not.

REGINA: Not even for a bit of fabric for a dress, just this once?

ENGSTRAND: Come to town with me and you'll have all the dresses you want.

REGINA: Pah – I can do that myself.

ENGSTRAND: But it'll be better with a father's guiding hand, Regina. I can get us a nice house on Little Harbour Street. They don't want much of a deposit – and we could make it into a sort of sailor's hostel, you know.

REGINA: But I'm not going to live with you. I don't want anything to do with you. Now, go away.

ENGSTRAND: You wouldn't be damn well living with me for long, my girl – not if you play your cards right. Handle yourself well. A pretty young lass like you...

REGINA: Well – ?

ENGSTRAND: It wouldn't be long before an officer turned up – a ship's captain, maybe.

REGINA: I don't want to marry someone like that. Sailors have no savoir-vivre.

ENGSTRAND: What don't they have?

REGINA: I know what sailors are like. They're not husband material.

ENGSTRAND: Well, don't marry them, then. It can still pay.

More confidentially.

That fellow – that Englishman – the one with the yacht – he gave her three hundred kroner, and she was no prettier than you.

REGINA: *(Going towards him.)* Get out of here.

ENGSTRAND: *(Stepping back.)* Hey – you wouldn't hit me, would you?

REGINA: Yes. If you talk about my mother like that. Go on, get out.

Pushes him up to the garden door.

And don't slam the door. Master Alving –

ENGSTRAND: Is asleep – I know. Funny how worried you are about Master Alving.

Quieter.

It's not possible that he's – ?

REGINA: Oh, get out of here, quick. You're talking nonsense. No, not that way, Pastor Manders is coming. Down the kitchen stairs.

ENGSTRAND: *(Moving towards the right.)* Alright, alright. But you have a chat with him. He'll tell you what a child owes her father. For I am your father, you know, it says so in the Register.

He goes through the door that REGINA has opened. She shuts it, checks herself in the mirror, fans herself with her handkerchief and straightens her collar. She then busies herself with the plants. MANDERS enters through the conservatory. He wears an overcoat, carries an umbrella, and has a small travelling bag slung over his shoulder.

MANDERS: Good afternoon, Miss Engstrand.

REGINA: *(Turning round with a look of pleased surprise.)* Oh, good afternoon, Pastor Manders. Has the steamer arrived?

MANDERS: It's just in.

Comes into the room.

Dreadful, this rain.

REGINA: *(Following him in.)* A blessing for the farmers, Pastor.

MANDERS: You're right there. We townsfolk don't think about things like that.

Begins to take off his overcoat.

REGINA: Here, let me help you. There now. It's soaked through, I'll hang it in the hall. And your umbrella. I'll leave it open to dry.

She leaves by the door on the right. MANDERS puts his hat and bag down on a chair. REGINA re-enters.

MANDERS: Oh, it's good to be indoors. So, all's well here on the estate?

REGINA: Yes, thanks.

MANDERS: Very busy, though, I imagine, getting everything ready for tomorrow?

REGINA: Oh, yes, there's plenty to do.

MANDERS: And Mrs Alving's at home, I trust?

REGINA: Oh, yes, she's just gone upstairs, to take the young master his chocolate.

MANDERS: Oh yes, I heard down at the pier that Osvald had come home.

REGINA: Yes, the day before yesterday. We didn't expect him back until today.

MANDERS: Fit and well, I hope?

REGINA: Yes, thank you, he seems to be. But exhausted. He came straight from Paris, non-stop. He's having a nap, I think, so let's talk quietly, if you don't mind.

MANDERS: Very quiet.

REGINA: *(While she moves an armchair to the table.)* Do sit down, Pastor, and make yourself at home.

He sits down; she puts a footstool under his feet.

There. Is the Pastor comfortable?

MANDERS: Very.

Looks at her.

You know, Miss Engstrand, I do believe you've grown since I saw you last.

REGINA: Really? Madam says I've – filled out.

MANDERS: Filled out? Maybe a little – quite properly, of course.

A short pause.

REGINA: Shall I tell Madam you're here?

MANDERS: No hurry, child. So, Regina, my dear, how has your father been getting on?

REGINA: Pretty well, Pastor, thank you.

MANDERS: He came to see me the last time he was in town.

REGINA: Did he! He always enjoys a talk with the Pastor.

MANDERS: I suppose you've seen him regularly?

REGINA: Me? Oh – yes, if I have the time.

MANDERS: Your father's not a very strong character, Miss Engstrand, is he? He needs a guiding hand.

REGINA: I know.

MANDERS: Someone to cling on to, someone whose judgment he can rely on. He said so himself, the last time he came to see me.

REGINA: He said something like that to me too. But I don't think Mrs Alving could manage without me – especially with the new orphanage. And I'd hate to leave her. She's always been so kind to me.

MANDERS: But a daughter's duty, dear child – Of course, we'd have to get her permission.

REGINA: Still, I don't think it's right, at my age, to keep house for a single man.

MANDERS: But, dear Miss Engstrand, it's your own father we're talking about.

REGINA: Maybe, but all the same – I mean if it was a decent house, with a real gentleman –

MANDERS: But my dear Regina.

REGINA: – someone I could care for, be like a daughter to...

MANDERS: Come, come, dear child –

REGINA: Because I'd really like to live in town. It's so lonely out here and, well, Pastor Manders, you know what it's like to be all alone in the world. And, though I say so myself, I really am very capable. Can't the Pastor think of somewhere suitable?

MANDERS: Me? No.

REGINA: But, my dear Pastor – please don't forget about me, if –

MANDERS getting up.

No, Miss Engstrand, I won't.

REGINA: Because, if I –

MANDERS: Perhaps you'd go and fetch Mrs Alving?

REGINA: Yes, Pastor, at once.

She goes out left. MANDERS walks up and down the room a couple of times, stands for a moment with his hands behind his back and looks out into the garden. Then he comes back to the table, picks up a book and reads the title page, is shocked and looks at the others.

MANDERS: Hm – Really.

MRS ALVING comes in by the door on the left. She's followed by REGINA, who goes out again through the second door on the right.

MRS ALVING: *(Holding out her hand.)* Pastor Manders, welcome.

MANDERS: Good afternoon, Mrs Alving. Well, here I am, as promised.

MRS ALVING: Always punctual.

MANDERS: It was hard to get away. What with all those committees and so forth –

MRS ALVING: All the kinder of you to come so promptly. We can get our business done before dinner. But where are your bags?

MANDERS: *(Quickly.)* They're down at the store. I'll stay there tonight.

MRS ALVING: *(Repressing a smile.)* I can't persuade you to stay here this time either?

MANDERS: Oh no, Mrs Alving, thanks all the same. I'll go there, as usual. It's so convenient, for the steamer, you know.

MRS ALVING: As you like. But it's so different now, two oldies like us –

MANDERS: Ha, ha. You will have your little joke. But, of course, you're in high spirits today – what with the celebrations tomorrow and then Osvald's back too, isn't he?

MRS ALVING: Yes, aren't I lucky? It's more than two years since he was last home, and he's promised to stay the winter.

MANDERS: Really? What a good son he is. There must be so many attractions in Paris and Rome.

MRS ALVING: Yes, but he has his mother here, you see. Bless the dear boy, there's still a corner in his heart for his mother.

MANDERS: It would be tragic if being away from home and following his artistic calling were to dull his natural affections.

MRS ALVING: There's no danger of that, I'm happy to say. I wonder if you'll recognise him. He'll be down soon. He's just having a rest on the sofa upstairs. But do sit down, dear Pastor.

MANDERS: Thank you. You're sure it's convenient?

MRS ALVING: Of course.

She sits down at the table.

MANDERS: Good. Then let me show you –

He goes to the chair where his bag is and takes out a folder. He sits on the opposite side of the table and looks for somewhere to put the papers.

Now, first of all, here's –

Breaks off.

Tell me, Mrs Alving, what are these books doing here?

MRS ALVING: I'm reading them.

MANDERS: Do you often read books like these?

MRS ALVING: Certainly.

MANDERS: Do you feel any better or happier for reading them?

MRS ALVING: I feel reassured.

MANDERS: How strange. Why's that?

MRS ALVING: Well, they explain – they confirm – many of the things I've been thinking about. You know, what surprises me, Pastor, is that there's really nothing new in them. Just what most people think and believe already. But either they don't say it or won't admit it.

MANDERS: Good Lord, do you seriously believe that most people – ?

MRS ALVING: Yes, I do.

MANDERS: Not in the countryside, surely? Not out here?

MRS ALVING: Here too.

MANDERS: Well, really –

MRS ALVING: What's your objection to them?

MANDERS: My objection? You surely don't think I waste my time reading books like these?

MRS ALVING: So, in other words, you have no idea what it is you're condemning?

MANDERS: I've read enough about them to disapprove of them.

MRS ALVING: Yes, but what's your own opinion –

MANDERS: My dear Mrs Alving, there are some occasions in life when one should rely on the opinion of others. That's the way the world works, and quite right too. What would happen to society otherwise?

MRS ALVING: Exactly.

MANDERS: I can't deny that such books have appeal. And I don't blame you for wanting to explore the ideas that are, I gather, current in the wider world – where you've let your son roam for so long. But –

MRS ALVING: But – ?

MANDERS: *(Lowering his voice.)* One doesn't talk about it, Mrs Alving. One certainly doesn't talk in public about what one reads and considers in the privacy of one's own home.

MRS ALVING: I agree.

MANDERS: And you should think of your obligations to this orphanage – which you founded when your views on such matters were – as far as I know – quite different.

MRS ALVING: Absolutely. But it was the orphanage...

MANDERS: That we were going to talk about, yes. But discretion, dear lady, please... Now, down to business.

Opens an envelope and takes out some papers.

Do you see these?

MRS ALVING: The deeds?

MANDERS: Yes, all of them, in order. It's been hard assembling them in time, I can tell you. I had to lean on the authorities, they're so cautious. But here they are.

Turns over the papers.

This is the deed of conveyance for that part of the Rosenvold estate known as 'The Sunlit Bay', along with the buildings newly erected thereon – the school, the teachers' homes and the chapel. And here are the articles for the endowment of the institution. Look –

Reads.

'Statutes for the Captain Alving Memorial Orphanage.'

MRS ALVING: *(After a long look at the papers.)* So.

MANDERS: I thought 'Captain' was better than 'Court Chamberlain.' Less ostentatious.

MRS ALVING: As you wish.

MANDERS: And here is the statement for the capital, with the interest set aside for the running costs.

MRS ALVING: Many thanks. Would you keep hold of them?

MANDERS: With pleasure. I think it's best to leave the money in the bank for now. The interest rate isn't good, it's true: four per cent at six months' notice. Later, if we can find a decent mortgage – it would have to be a first one, of course, with impeccable security – we can reconsider.

MRS ALVING: Yes, yes, dear Manders, you know best.

MANDERS: I'll keep an eye out, anyway. But there's one thing I've been meaning to ask.

MRS ALVING: What's that?

MANDERS: Is the orphanage to be insured?

MRS ALVING: Of course.

MANDERS: One moment. Think carefully.

MRS ALVING: Everything I own is insured – buildings and contents, crops, livestock – everything.

MANDERS: Naturally. They're your property. I do the same. But, you see, this is different. The orphanage is, so to speak, consecrated to a higher use.

MRS ALVING: Yes, but –

MANDERS: Personally, I don't see any objection to insuring yourself against risk –

MRS ALVING: Exactly.

MANDERS: – but what about opinion around here? You know better than I do, of course.

MRS ALVING: What opinion – ?

MANDERS: Is there a body of opinion   significant opinion, I mean – that might be shocked by it?

MRS ALVING: What do you mean: significant opinion?

MANDERS: Well, people whose opinions matter.

MRS ALVING: There are dozens, who might –

MANDERS: That's just it. There are many of them in town, too. Every congregation has them. Well, they might conclude that we showed insufficient faith in divine providence.

MRS ALVING: But, dear Pastor, you don't think you're –

MANDERS: Oh, my conscience is clear. But we wouldn't be able to stop it being misinterpreted. And that might harm the orphanage.

MRS ALVING: Well, if that's the case –

MANDERS: Nor can I overlook the difficult – embarrassing even – position that I'd be placed in. This orphanage is attracting a great deal of attention. It's been built to benefit the town, and people hope that it'll lower their taxes. But I worry that, as your adviser, the zealots might blame me most of all.

MRS ALVING: You mustn't expose yourself to that.

MANDERS: Not to mention the attacks that would, no doubt, appear in certain magazines and periodicals, which would –

MRS ALVING: Not another word, dear Pastor, that settles it.

MANDERS: So you don't want it insured?

MRS ALVING: No, leave it as it is.

MANDERS: *(Leaning back in his chair.)* But if there was an accident – you can never tell – could you make good the damage?

MRS ALVING: Of course not.

MANDERS: So, Mrs Alving, this is a major liability we're taking on.

MRS ALVING: But what else can we do?

MANDERS: That's just it. We can't. We mustn't expose ourselves to misinterpretation, and we have no right to offend the congregation.

MRS ALVING: You mustn't, as a clergyman, at any rate.

MANDERS: But I'm sure the institution will be attended by good fortune – that it will be under special protection.

MRS ALVING: Let's hope so, Pastor Manders.

MANDERS: So is that settled?

MRS ALVING: Certainly.

MANDERS: As you wish.

Makes a note.

No insurance, then.

MRS ALVING: It's odd that you mentioned this today –

MANDERS: I've been meaning to ask you for a while.

MRS ALVING: – because we nearly had a fire over there yesterday.

MANDERS: Really?

MRS ALVING: It was nothing really – just some shavings in the carpentry shop caught fire.

MANDERS: Where Engstrand works?

MRS ALVING: Yes. He's often careless with matches apparently.

MANDERS: He has so much on his mind, poor chap – temptations. I gather he's determined to live a better life.

MRS ALVING: Who told you that?

MANDERS: He did. And he's a good workman too.

MRS ALVING: When he's sober.

MANDERS: Yes, yes, his little weakness. But the pain in his leg drives him to it, he says. The last time he was in town, I was really quite touched. He thanked me for finding him work out here, so he could be near his Regina –

MRS ALVING: I don't think he sees much of her.

MANDERS: He speaks to her every day, he said.

MRS ALVING: Perhaps he does.

MANDERS: He says he needs someone who can hold him back when temptation strikes. That's the good thing about Jacob Engstrand, the way he turns up so helpless, full of guilt and confessing to his frailty. The last time we had a talk... Look, Mrs Alving, suppose he needed Regina back home with him –

MRS ALVING: *(Standing up suddenly.)* Regina?

MANDERS: – you mustn't stand in his way.

MRS ALVING: I most certainly will. Besides, Regina is to have a position in the orphanage, as well you know.

MANDERS: But he's her father –

MRS ALVING: Oh, I know what kind of father he's been to her. No, not with my consent.

MANDERS: *(Getting up.)* Dear Mrs Alving, don't be rash. It's sad the way you underestimate poor old Engstrand. It's as if you were scared...

MRS ALVING: *(More calmly.)* That's not the point. I've taken Regina into my home, and there she stays.

Listens.

Ssh, dear Pastor, let's not talk about it anymore.

Her face lights up.

Listen. There's Osvald coming down the stairs. Let's just think about him now.

OSVALD ALVING, in a light overcoat, hat in hand and smoking a large meerschaum pipe, comes in by the door on the left.

OSVALD: *(Standing in the doorway.)* Oh, I beg your pardon – I thought you were in the office.

Comes in.

Good afternoon, Pastor.

MANDERS: *(Staring at him.)* How extraordinary.

MRS ALVING: Well, what do you think, Pastor Manders?

MANDERS: I – I think – is it really – ?

OSVALD: Yes, the Prodigal Son.

MANDERS: My dear fellow –

OSVALD: Or rather, the son who's returned home.

MRS ALVING: Osvald's thinking of the way you were so opposed to him becoming an artist.

MANDERS: Well, many steps seem unwise at first, that later –

Grasps his hand.

But welcome home, Osvald. Really, my dear fellow – may I call you by your first name?

OSVALD: Of course, what else?

MANDERS: Excellent. What I mean, dear Osvald, is that you mustn't think I condemn the artist's life. I'm sure there are many artists who keep the inner man free from harm.

OSVALD: Let's hope so.

MRS ALVING: *(Beaming with pleasure.)* I know one who's kept both inner and outer man free from harm. Just look at him, Pastor.

OSVALD: *(Wanders across the room.)* Alright, mother dear, let's change the subject.

MANDERS: You can't deny it. And you've begun to make a name for yourself too. You're often in the papers – favourably too. Though, I must admit, not so much nowadays.

OSVALD: *(Going towards the conservatory.)* I've not done much painting recently.

MRS ALVING: Even an artist must rest sometimes.

MANDERS: I'm sure. To gather his strength for even greater efforts.

OSVALD: Yes... Mother, will dinner be ready soon?

MRS ALVING: In half an hour, at the most. He has a good appetite, thank heavens.

MANDERS: And a taste for tobacco.

OSVALD: I found Father's pipe in the room upstairs –

MANDERS: Ah, so that's what it was.

MRS ALVING: What?

MANDERS: When Osvald came in with that pipe in his mouth, I thought his father had come back from the dead.

OSVALD: Really?

MRS ALVING: How can you say that? Osvald takes after me.

MANDERS: Yes, but there's something about the corners of his mouth – his lips – that reminds me of Captain Alving – especially when he smokes.

MRS ALVING: No, no. I think Osvald has more of a clergyman's mouth.

MANDERS: Well, yes – many of my colleagues have a similar expression.

MRS ALVING: Put the pipe down, dear boy. I don't like smoking in here.

OSVALD: *(Puts down his pipe.)* All right, I just wanted to try it. I smoked it once when I was a child.

MRS ALVING: Really?

OSVALD: Yes, as a young boy. I remember going up to father's room one evening. He was in such a good mood.

MRS ALVING: Oh, you can't remember anything about those days.

OSVALD: Yes, distinctly, he put me on his lap and made me smoke his pipe. 'Smoke, boy,' he said, 'have a good old smoke.' And I smoked as hard as I could, but turned pale and sweated like a pig. And then he roared with laughter.

MANDERS: What an odd thing to do.

MRS ALVING: Osvald just dreamt it.

OSVALD: No, mother, it wasn't a dream. Because then – don't you remember? – you came in and dragged me off to the nursery. And I was sick, and you were crying. Did father often play tricks like that?

MANDERS: As a young man he was full of tricks –

OSVALD: But he did so much – which was good and useful, I mean – despite dying so young.

MANDERS: My dear Osvald Alving, you bear the name of a hard working and virtuous man. Let's hope it'll inspire you further.

OSVALD: It should do, yes.

MANDERS: In any case it was good of you to come home to honour his memory.

OSVALD: It was the least I could do.

MRS ALVING: And letting me keep him here for so long – that's the best thing of all.

MANDERS: Yes, I gather you're going to spend the winter here?

OSVALD: I'm staying indefinitely, Pastor Manders – Oh, it's so good to be home again.

MRS ALVING: *(Beaming.)* Isn't it?

MANDERS: *(Looking sympathetically at him.)* You went out into the world very early, my dear Osvald.

OSVALD: Yes. I sometimes wonder if it wasn't too early.

MRS ALVING: Not a bit of it. It's best for an active boy, especially an only child. He shouldn't be stuck at home with his parents getting spoiled.

MANDERS: That's debatable, Mrs Alving. A child's place is, and always must be, in his father's house.

OSVALD: There I agree with the Pastor.

MANDERS: Take your son. Yes, we can talk like this in front of him. What have been the consequences? He's twenty-six, twenty-seven, and has never known a well-regulated home.

OSVALD: Excuse me, Pastor Manders, there you're wrong.

MANDERS: Really? I thought you'd lived exclusively in artistic circles.

OSVALD: I have.

MANDERS: And mostly with younger artists.

OSVALD: Certainly.

MANDERS: But I thought that people like that, as a rule, can't afford to have a family and start a home.

OSVALD: Many of them can't afford to marry, Pastor Manders.

MANDERS: That's my point.

OSVALD: But they can still have a home. And many do. Good, comfortable homes, too.

MRS ALVING, who has listened carefully, nods in agreement, but says nothing.

MANDERS: But I'm not talking about bachelors. By a home I mean family life – a man living with his wife and children.

OSVALD: Or with his children and his children's mother.

MANDERS: *(Starts and clasps his hands.)* Good Lord.

OSVALD: What's wrong?

MANDERS: Living with his children's mother?

OSVALD: Would you rather he turned his back on her?

MANDERS: You're talking about illegal relationships. Sham marriages.

OSVALD: I've never seen anything sham in these people's lives.

MANDERS: But d'you mean that even a moderately well brought up young man or woman can reconcile themselves to such a life – and make no secret of it?

OSVALD: What else can they do? A poor young artist, and a girl – it costs money to get married. What can they do?

MANDERS: What can they do? Well, Master Alving, I'll tell you what they should do. They should stay away from each other in the first place – that's what they should do.

OSVALD: That wouldn't have much effect on hot-blooded young people in love.

MRS ALVING: Exactly.

MANDERS: *(Persistently.)* And to think that the authorities tolerate such things. That it's permitted in public.

Turns to MRS ALVING.

Was I so wrong to worry about your son? In circles where immorality is rampant – where, you could say, it's almost de rigeur –

OSVALD: Let me tell you something, Pastor Manders. I've been a frequent Sunday guest at some of these 'irregular' households.

MANDERS: On Sundays, too?

OSVALD: The day of rest, yes. But I've never heard one offensive word, still less seen anything that could be called immoral. But do you know where I have observed immorality in artists' circles?

MANDERS: No, thank heavens, I don't.

OSVALD: Well, I'll tell you. When one of your model husbands and fathers comes for a look around, and does the artists the honour of visiting them in their garrets. Then we learn something, I can tell you. They tell us about places and sights we'd never even dreamt of.

MANDERS: What? Are you saying that gentlemen from here, when they're away from home – ?

OSVALD: Haven't you heard them complain about the immorality abroad, when they come home?

MANDERS: Yes, of course, but –

MRS ALVING: I've heard them, too.

OSVALD: Well, take their word for it. They're experts.

Putting his hands to his head.

To think that our beautiful way of life should be so sullied.

MRS ALVING: You mustn't get worked up, Osvald. It doesn't help.

OSVALD: No, you're right, mother. Besides, it isn't good for me. I'm so tired. I'll take a little walk before dinner. Forgive me, Pastor Manders. I'm sure you don't understand, but that's the way I feel.

Goes out by the second door on the right.

MRS ALVING: My poor boy.

MANDERS: Indeed. So, this is what he's come to.

MRS ALVING looks at him, but doesn't speak.

He called himself the Prodigal Son. It's all too true, alas.

MRS ALVING looks steadily at him.

And what do you say about all this?

MRS ALVING: I agree with everything Osvald said.

MANDERS: Agree? With thinking like that?

MRS ALVING: I've come to the same conclusions, Pastor Manders, out here. I've never dared speak about it. But I don't need to now: my son will speak for me.

MANDERS: Mrs Alving, you deserve our deepest sympathy. But now I must have a serious word with you. I no longer stand here as your adviser and executor, as you and your late husband's friend. No, I stand here as your priest, just as I did when you went astray.

MRS ALVING: And what does my priest have to say to me?

MANDERS: First, Mrs Alving, let me refresh your memory. This is the perfect moment to do so. Tomorrow is the tenth anniversary of your husband's death; tomorrow a memorial to him will be unveiled; tomorrow I will address the flock. But today I want to speak to you alone.

MRS ALVING: Very well, Pastor Manders, speak.

MANDERS: Have you forgotten that after just a year of married life you stood on the edge of an abyss? That you abandoned house and home? That you ran away from your husband – yes, Mrs Alving, ran away – and refused to go back, whatever he said?

MRS ALVING: Have you forgotten how unhappy I was during that first year?

MANDERS: To pursue happiness in this world is to be governed by the spirit of rebellion. What right do we have to happiness? No, we must do our duty, Mrs Alving. And your duty was to cleave to the man you'd chosen and to whom you were tied by a sacred bond.

MRS ALVING: You know the kind of life my husband was living at the time – his excesses.

MANDERS: I know the rumours, and I'd be the last person to approve of his behaviour before he was married, if true.

But it's not a wife's role to judge her husband. It was your duty, in all humility, to bear the cross that a higher power had laid on you, for your own good. But you shrugged it off and deserted the man whose stumbling footsteps you should have helped. You risked your good name, and almost wrecked the good name of others.

MRS ALVING: Others? One other, don't you mean?

MANDERS: It was utterly thoughtless of you to seek refuge with me.

MRS ALVING: Our priest? Our family friend?

MANDERS: All the more reason. You should thank God I had the necessary fortitude – that I turned you away, and was given the strength of mind to lead you back on the path of duty, and home to your lawful wedded husband.

MRS ALVING: Yes, Pastor Manders, that was your doing.

MANDERS: I was just the humble instrument of a higher power. But isn't it true that by placing the yoke of duty and obedience back on your shoulders I sowed seeds that would sustain you for the rest of your life? Didn't things turn out as I said they would? Didn't Alving come back to you, as a man should? Didn't he live a life of love and fidelity for the rest of his day's? Didn't he become a benefactor to the community? And didn't he raise you up to his level, so you gradually became his helper – and a fine one, too. I know, Mrs Alving, I know, and for that I give you praise. But now I come to your second grave error.

MRS ALVING: And what's that?

MANDERS: Just as you once denied your duties as a wife, so, since then, you've denied them as a mother.

MRS ALVING: Ah –

MANDERS: You've been willful all your life. You've always been drawn to the uncontrolled and the reckless. You've never accepted any kind of restraint. Anything that seemed unpleasant, you tossed carelessly to one side, as if it were a burden. You got tired of being a wife, so you left your husband. And your duties as a mother were hard, so you packed your child off to live among strangers.

MRS ALVING: That's true, I did.

MANDERS: And so you've became a stranger to him.

MRS ALVING: No, I haven't, no.

MANDERS: You have, you must have. And look how he's returned. Think carefully, Mrs Alving. You sinned against your husband – you admit as much, by erecting this memorial to him. But now you should admit how much you've sinned against your son. There may be time to save him from the path of wickedness. Mend your ways, and reform what can be reformed. Because, Mrs Alving, the truth is –

With a raised finger.

– you are a guilty mother. I consider it my duty to tell you.

A short silence.

MRS ALVING: *(Speaking slowly and with self-control.)* You've spoken, Pastor Manders, and tomorrow you'll make a speech in memory of my husband. I won't say anything tomorrow. But I want to speak to you now, the way you've spoken to me.

MANDERS: Please do. You want to make your excuses.

MRS ALVING: No. I want to tell you something –

MANDERS: Well?

MRS ALVING: Everything you said about my husband and me, and our life together after you had – as you put it – led me back onto the path of duty: well, you know nothing about it. You never set foot in our house again – you, our companion, our family friend.

MANDERS: Remember that you and your husband moved out of town soon afterwards.

MRS ALVING: Yes, and you never came to visit us while he was alive. It was just setting up the orphanage that made you visit me after he'd died.

MANDERS: *(In a low and uncertain voice,)* Helen – if that's meant as a reproach, I beg you to consider –

MRS ALVING: – the respect I owe the cloth? – yes. And because I was a runaway wife. You can never be too careful with such women.

MANDERS: Good Lord – Mrs Alving, you exaggerate wildly.

MRS ALVING: Maybe. All I mean is that when you pass judgment on my behaviour as a wife you have nothing to go on but gossip.

MANDERS: Maybe. Well?

MRS ALVING: Well, Pastor Manders, I'm going to tell you the truth. I swore to myself that you should hear it one day – you, and you alone.

MANDERS: And what is this truth?

MRS ALVING: The truth is that my husband died just as debauched as he had been all his life.

MANDERS: *(Feeling for a chair.)* What?

MRS ALVING: After nineteen years of marriage, he was just as debauched – in his desires, at least – as he was before you married us.

MANDERS: And you call his youthful indiscretions – his excesses, if you like – debauchery?

MRS ALVING: That's what his doctor called them.

MANDERS: I don't understand.

MRS ALVING: You don't need to.

MANDERS: I'm confused. Are you saying that your marriage – all those years of married life – was nothing but secret misery?

MRS ALVING: I am. So now you know.

MANDERS: This – astonishes me. I don't understand. How could it stay secret?

MRS ALVING: That's what I fought for, every day. When Osvald was born, I saw a slight improvement. But it didn't last long. And after that, I had to fight twice as hard – so no one would know what kind of man his father was. You know how charming Alving could be; people couldn't believe anything but good of him. He was the kind of man whose behaviour has no effect on his reputation. But finally, Pastor Manders – and you must hear this – something terrible happened.

MANDERS: Worse than what you've already told me.

MRS ALVING: Yes, I'd put up with it all, even though I knew what he got up to when he was away from home. But when scandal entered these four walls –

MANDERS: What do you mean? Here?

MRS ALVING: Yes, in our own home. I was in there –

Pointing to the near door on the right.

– in the dining-room, when I found out. I was busy and the door was ajar. I heard the maid come up from the garden to water the plants.

MANDERS: And then – ?

MRS ALVING: My husband joined her. And whispered something in her ear. And then –

With a short laugh.

– oh, I can still hear it – it's heartbreaking, humiliating – my own maid said: 'Let me go, sir. Let me go.'

MANDERS: Oh, my dear. But that was just foolishness, Mrs Alving, surely.

MRS ALVING: I soon found out. The Court Chamberlain had his way with the maid – and that had its consequences, Pastor Manders.

MANDERS: *(As if turned to stone.)* And all of that here? In this house!

MRS ALVING: I've put up with a great deal in this house, to keep him at home in the evenings – and at night – I had to watch him drinking in his room up there. I sat with him, just the two of us, drinking, listening to his filth, and wrestling him into his bed –

MANDERS: *(Trembling.)* And you put up with that?

MRS ALVING: For my son's sake. But the final insult, when my own maid – well, I decided to put an end to it. I took control – both of him and others. I had a weapon to use against him, you see, and he didn't dare say anything. And that was when Osvald was sent away. He was nearly seven, and was beginning to notice things and ask questions, as children do. I couldn't bear it. It was as if my child would be poisoned by the air of this polluted house. So that's why I sent him away. And now you see why I didn't let him set foot in this place while his father was still alive. No one knows what that's cost me.

MANDERS: How terrible.

MRS ALVING: I wouldn't have survived if I didn't have my work. Yes, I've worked. All the innovations on the estate, the improvements that brought my husband such honour – do you think he could be bothered with it? No, he used to lie about all day reading an old Court Circular. And I'll tell you this too: it was me who got him going when he was sober; it was me who put up with it when he was drunk and felt sorry for himself.

MANDERS: And this is the man to whom you're building a memorial.

MRS ALVING: So now you see the power of a bad conscience.

MANDERS: A bad – ? What do you mean?

MRS ALVING: I was always worried that the truth would come out and be believed. And that's why the orphanage has been built, to silence the rumours and get rid of any doubt.

MANDERS: You've certainly not fallen short there, Mrs Alving.

MRS ALVING: I had another reason too. I didn't want Osvald, my own son, to inherit anything at all from his father.

MANDERS: So, in fact, it's Captain Alving's money that –

MRS ALVING: Yes. The payments that, every year, I've given towards the fund, are exactly the same amount – I counted it carefully – which once made Lieutenant Alving such 'a good catch'.

MANDERS: I see.

MRS ALVING: That was my purchase price. I don't want that left to Osvald. Everything my son inherits will come from me.

OSVALD comes in by the far door on the right. He has left his hat and coat outside.

MRS ALVING: Back again, darling boy?

OSVALD: Yes, what can you do in this endless rain? I gather dinner's nearly ready. Excellent.

REGINA comes in from the dining-room, carrying a parcel.

REGINA: This has just arrived, ma'am.

Gives it to her.

MRS ALVING: *(Glancing at MANDERS.)* The hymn sheets for tomorrow, I expect.

MANDERS: Hm –

REGINA: And dinner is served.

MRS ALVING: Good. We'll come in a moment. I just want to –

Begins to open the parcel.

REGINA: *(To OSVALD.)* White wine or red, sir?

OSVALD: Both, please, Miss Engstrand.

REGINA: Bien – very well, Master Alving.

Goes into the dining-room.

OSVALD: I'd better help with the bottles

Follows her into the dining-room, leaving the door ajar.

MRS ALVING: I thought so. The hymn sheets, Pastor Manders.

MANDERS: *(Clasping his hands.)* How can I make my speech tomorrow –

MRS ALVING: Oh, you'll find a way, I'm sure.

MANDERS: *(In a low voice, fearing to be heard in the dining-room.)* Yes, we mustn't raise any suspicions.

MRS ALVING: *(Quietly but firmly.)* No, and then this ghastly farce can finally come to an end. The day after tomorrow, it'll be as if the dead never lived in this house. There'll be nobody here but my son and his mother.

From the dining-room the sound of a chair being knocked over.

REGINA: *(In a loud whisper.)* Osvald. Are you mad? Let me go.

MRS ALVING: *(Starting in horror.)* Ah –

She stares wildly at the half-open door. OSVALD is heard coughing, and then humming. A bottle is uncorked.

MANDERS: *(Agitated.)* What was that? What is it, Mrs Alving?

MRS ALVING: *(Hoarsely.)* Ghosts. The two of them in the conservatory – they're back.

MANDERS: What are you saying. Regina – ? Is she – ?

MRS ALVING: Yes. Come. Not a word –

Grips MANDERS by the arm and walks unsteadily with him into the dining-room.

ACT TWO

The landscape is obscured by mist. MANDERS and MRS ALVING come in from the dining-room.

MRS ALVING: *(In the doorway.)* You're welcome, Pastor. Osvald, aren't you going to join us?

OSVALD: No, thanks. I'll go out for a walk, I think.

MRS ALVING: Yes, do. The weather's clearing up a bit.

She shuts the dining-room door, then goes to the hall door and calls.

Regina.

REGINA: *(From without.)* Yes, ma'am?

MRS ALVING: Go down to the pantry and help with the decorations, would you?

REGINA: Yes, ma'am.

MRS ALVING makes sure that she has gone and then shuts the door.

MANDERS: He can't hear anything in there, can he?

MRS ALVING: Not when the door's shut. Besides, he's going out.

MANDERS: I'm utterly bewildered. I don't know how I managed to eat any of your excellent dinner.

MRS ALVING: *(Walking up and down, trying to control her agitation.)* Nor me. But what's to be done?

MANDERS: Yes, what's to be done? To tell you the truth, I've no idea. I've no experience of things like this.

MRS ALVING: I'm sure nothing serious has happened yet.

MANDERS: God forbid. But it's quite inappropriate, whatever.

MRS ALVING: It's just a silly joke of Osvald's, I'm sure.

MANDERS: Well, as I say, I'm inexperienced in such things. But it seems to me that whatever happens –

MRS ALVING: She must leave – at once. That's clear –

MANDERS: Absolutely clear.

MRS ALVING. But where to? We can't –

MANDERS: Where to? Back to her father, of course.

MRS ALVING: Who did you say?

MANDERS: Her – Oh, but, of course, Engstrand isn't her father – Good God, Mrs Alving, how can this be possible? You must be wrong, surely.

MRS ALVING: Unfortunately not, more's the pity. Joanna, the maid, confessed it – and Alving couldn't deny it. So it had to be hushed up.

MANDERS: Of course.

MRS ALVING: She left immediately, with a good sum of money to make her hold her tongue. She sorted it all out herself. She renewed her old acquaintance with Engstrand; she must have hinted at how much money she had, and cooked up some story about a foreigner who'd been here in the summer in his yacht. And she and Engstrand were married in a hurry. Remember, you married them yourself.

MANDERS: I just don't understand – I remember Engstrand coming to arrange the wedding. He was so penitent about it all.

MRS ALVING: Well, he had to take the blame.

MANDERS: But the lies. And with me, too. I really wouldn't have believed it of Jacob Engstrand. Well, I'll have to give him a good talking to. And the immorality of it all. For money – How much did the maid have?

MRS ALVING: Three hundred kroner.

MANDERS: Imagine – marrying a fallen woman for three hundred kroner.

MRS ALVING: What about me? Marrying a fallen man.

MANDERS: Good God. What are you saying? A fallen man?

MRS ALVING: Do you think my husband was any purer when I married him than Joanna was when Engstrand met her at the altar?

MANDERS: That's different.

MRS ALVING: Not that different. A difference in price: three hundred kroner as opposed to an entire fortune.

MANDERS: How can you compare such things? You listened to your heart – and your family.

MRS ALVING: *(Looking away from him.)* I thought you knew where 'my heart' was in those days.

MANDERS: *(In a constrained voice.)* If I'd known anything of the sort, I wouldn't have been a frequent guest in your husband's house.

MRS ALVING: Well, the fact remains that I didn't listen to myself.

MANDERS: You listened to your close relatives, as is right and proper – your mother, your aunts.

MRS ALVING: True. The three of them totted it all up. It's incredible how quickly they decided it would be mad to reject his offer. If mother could see what all that money led to.

MANDERS: No one is responsible for the outcome. Anyway, the match was made according to the law.

MRS ALVING: *(Going to the window.)* Oh, the law, the law. I sometimes think that's the root of all misery in the world.

MANDERS: Mrs Alving, what a wicked thing to say.

MRS ALVING: Maybe, but I don't attach much importance to things like that any more. I can't. I've had to fight my way to freedom.

MANDERS: What do you mean?

MRS ALVING: *(Tapping on the window panes.)* I shouldn't have hidden my husband's behaviour. But I wasn't brave enough to do anything else – for my own sake, really. I was too much of a coward.

MANDERS: A coward?

MRS ALVING: If people had heard anything, they'd have said; 'Poor man, it's hardly surprising he's gone astray, his wife has deserted him.'

MANDERS: And they would have had some justification.

MRS ALVING: *(Looking fixedly at him.)* If I'd been the woman I should have been, I'd have taken Osvald aside and said: 'Listen, your father was debauched' –

MANDERS: Heavens above.

MRS ALVING: – and I'd have told him everything I've told you, the whole lot.

MANDERS: I'm really quite shocked, Mrs Alving.

MRS ALVING: I know. I know. I'm shocked myself.

Comes away from the window.

You see, I'm such a coward.

MANDERS: Is it cowardice to do your duty? Have you forgotten that a child should love and honour his father and mother?

MRS ALVING: Let's not generalize, shall we? Let's ask, instead, 'Should Osvald love and honour Chamberlain Alving?'

MANDERS: You're his mother – isn't there a voice inside that prevents you from destroying your son's ideals?

MRS ALVING: Yes, but what about the truth?

MANDERS: What about his ideals?

MRS ALVING: Oh – ideals, ideals. If only I weren't such a coward.

MANDERS: Don't turn your back on ideals, Mrs Alving – they'll take their revenge. Look at Osvald. He hasn't many

ideals, more's the pity. But I know he sees his father as
something of an ideal.

MRS ALVING: You're right.

MANDERS: And you encouraged that in your letters.

MRS ALVING: Yes, it was my duty. And that's why I lied to him
– year in, year out. Oh, what a coward I've been.

MANDERS: You built up a happy illusion in your son's
mind, Mrs Alving – and that's not something you should
underestimate.

MRS ALVING: Oh, who knows if it was a good thing to do –
But I refuse to put up with any nonsense with Regina. I'm
not going to let him ruin that poor girl's life.

MANDERS: Good God, no – that would be terrible.

MRS ALVING: If I knew he was serious, and that it would make
him happy –

MANDERS: What do you mean?

MRS ALVING: But it wouldn't. Regina isn't like that, sadly.

MANDERS: I still don't understand. What do you mean?

MRS ALVING: If I weren't such a wretched coward, I'd say:
'Marry her, or make any arrangement you like – but let
there be no more lies.'

MANDERS: Good Lord. Are you actually suggesting – that
they get married? It's unthinkable.

MRS ALVING: Unthinkable? Tell me the truth, Pastor Manders,
don't you think there are dozens of couples around here
just as closely related?

MANDERS: I don't understand you.

MRS ALVING: Yes, you do.

MANDERS: I suppose you're thinking of cases where – Well,
sadly, family life isn't always as innocent as it should be.

But as for the kind of thing you're suggesting – well, it's impossible to say. But for you, a mother, to let your –

MRS ALVING: But I don't want it, not for anything. That's exactly what I'm saying.

MANDERS: Because you're a coward, as you put it? But if you weren't – good God – how revolting.

MRS ALVING: Well, we're all descended from such a union, aren't we? And who was responsible for that, Pastor Manders?

MANDERS: I won't discuss such things with you, Mrs Alving; you're hardly in the right frame of mind. But to say that you're a coward –

MRS ALVING: Let me tell you what I mean. I'm scared. I'm haunted by ghosts.

MANDERS: What?

MRS ALVING: Yes, ghosts. When I heard Regina and Osvald in there, it was like ghosts. I sometimes think we're all ghosts, Pastor Manders. It's not just what we've inherited from our parents, but all sorts of dead ideas and dead beliefs. They're not alive inside us; but they're there all the same, and we can't get rid of them. When I pick up a newspaper, I see ghosts between the lines. There must be ghosts everywhere. The air is thick with them. And we're all so afraid of the light.

MANDERS: Ah – so that's the fruit of your reading. And fine fruit it's borne – those terrible freethinkers and their vile, seditious books.

MRS ALVING: You're wrong, my friend. You're the one who made me think, and I'm grateful to you for that.

MENDERS: Me?

MRS ALVING: Yes, by making me submit to what you called my duty and my obligations; by praising as right and proper what my whole soul revolted against. That's what

47

made me look at how your teachings had been made. I wanted to unpick just one thread but the whole fabric soon unraveled in my hands. And then I realised that it was machine-made.

MANDERS: *(Softly, and with feeling.)* Is that what I achieved by the hardest struggle of my life?

MRS ALVING: Call it rather your most miserable defeat.

MANDERS: It was my greatest victory, Helen, victory over myself.

MRS ALVING: It was a crime against both of us.

MANDERS: A crime? – a crime that I said 'Woman, go back to your lawful husband', when you came to me, crying, 'Here I am, take me.' Was that a crime?

MRS ALVING: I think it was.

MANDERS: We really don't understand each other.

MRS ALVING: Not anymore, no.

MANDERS: Never – not in my most private moments – have I ever thought of you as anything but another man's wife.

MRS ALVING: I wonder.

MANDERS: Helen –

MRS ALVING: It's so easy to forget who we were.

MANDERS: Not me. I'm the same as I've ever been.

MRS ALVING: *(Turns.)* Well – let's not talk about the old days any more. You're up to your eyes in committees and board meetings, while I'm here, fighting ghosts, both inside and out.

MANDERS: I can perhaps help you defeat the ones on the outside. After what I've heard today, I can't in all conscience let a vulnerable young woman stay in your house.

MRS ALVING: Wouldn't it be best to get her settled? – in a decent marriage, I mean.

MANDERS: Certainly. For her, at any rate. Regina is at an age – well, I don't understand these things, but –

MRS ALVING: Regina matured early.

MANDERS: Yes, didn't she? I remember thinking that she was strikingly mature – physically, at least – when I prepared her for Confirmation. But now, she has to go home. To her father's care – but, of course, Engstrand isn't her – To think he could lie to me like that.

A knock is heard at the hall door.

MRS ALVING: Who can that be? Come in.

ENGSTRAND, dressed in his Sunday best, appears in the doorway.

ENGSTRAND: I beg your pardon, but –

MANDERS: Aha. Hm.

MRS ALVING: Oh, it's you, Engstrand.

ENGSTRAND: None of the maids were around, so I took the liberty of knocking.

MRS ALVING: All right. Come in. Did you want to talk to me about something?

ENGSTRAND: *(Coming in.)* No, thanks all the same, ma'am. It was the Pastor I wanted a word with.

MANDERS: *(Walking up and down.)* Really? You want to speak to me?

ENGSTRAND: Aye, sir, I'd be much obliged –

MANDERS: *(Stopping in front of him.)* Well, may I ask what?

ENGSTRAND: It's like this, Pastor, we're being paid off down there – thanks very much, Mrs Alving. And now the work's finished, I thought it would be nice and fitting for all of us who've worked together so well to round things off with a little prayer meeting this evening.

MANDERS: Prayers? At the orphanage?

ENGSTRAND: Aye, but only if it's agreeable to the Pastor –

MANDERS: Certainly – but – hm –

ENGSTRAND: I've made a practice of sharing a few prayers down there myself each evening.

MRS ALVING: Have you?

ENGSTRAND: Yes, ma'am – now and again – as a little edification, so to speak. But I'm just an ordinary fellow, and haven't the gift – so I thought since Pastor Manders happened to be here, he might –

MANDERS: But, first, Engstrand, let me ask you a question. Are you in the right frame of mind? Is your conscience clear?

ENGSTRAND: God forgive me, Pastor, but I really don't think my conscience is worth talking about.

MANDERS: But that's exactly what we have to talk about. Well, what do you say?

ENGSTRAND: My conscience? Well – it is bad sometimes, of course.

MANDERS: So you admit it? Well, will you tell me then – no secrets now – what is your relationship to Regina?

MRS ALVING: *(Hastily.)* Pastor Manders.

MANDERS: *(Calming her.)* – Leave it to me.

ENGSTRAND: To Regina? You made me jump.

Looks at MRS ALVING.

Nothing's happened to Regina, has there?

MANDERS: Let's hope not. What is your relationship to her? You claim to be her father, don't you?

ENGSTRAND: *(Unsteadily.)* Hm – Well, the Pastor knows all about me and my poor Joanna, may she rest in peace.

MANDERS: No more lies. Your late wife made a full confession to Mrs Alving, before she left her service...

ENGSTRAND: What – d'you mean to say – ? After all this time?

MANDERS: It had to come out, Engstrand.

ENGSTRAND: She promised, on oath –

MANDERS: Did she take an oath?

ENGSTRAND: Well, no – she just gave me her word, as much as a woman can.

MANDERS: And for all these years you've hidden the truth from me – and I'd put such faith in you.

ENGSTRAND: I'm sorry to say I have, sir.

MANDERS: Did I deserve that, Engstrand? Haven't I always been ready to help you, in word and deed, as far as lay in my power? Well? Haven't I?

ENGSTRAND: Indeed, there's many a time I would have been in difficulty without you, sir.

MANDERS: And this is the way you repay me – by getting me to make false entries in the Register, and for years hiding from me information which you owed both me and the truth. Your conduct has been inexcusable, Engstrand, and it's all over between us.

ENGSTRAND: *(With a sigh.)* Well, I can understand that.

MANDERS: How can you possibly justify your actions?

ENGSTRAND: But should she have felt even more shame by talking about it? Suppose for a moment that your reverence was in the same predicament as my poor Joanna.

MANDERS: Me?

ENGSTRAND: Oh, sir, I don't mean exactly the same. I mean, suppose there was something your reverence was ashamed of in the eyes of the world, so to speak. We men mustn't judge a poor woman too harshly, Pastor.

MANDERS. I'm not. I'm blaming you.

ENGSTRAND: Will your reverence allow me one wee question?

MANDERS: Go on.

ENGSTRAND: Isn't it right and proper for a man to raise up the fallen?

MANDERS: Of course.

ENGSTRAND: And isn't a man bound to keep his word?

MANDERS: He certainly is, but –

ENGSTRAND: When Joanna got into trouble with that Englishman – maybe he was an American or a Russkie, as they call them – well, sir, she moved into town. She'd turned me down once or twice already, poor thing; she only had eyes for good-looking fellows in those days, and I had this problem with my leg. Well, your reverence will remember that I went into that saloon bar where sailors were partying, drunkenness and intoxication, as they say. And that when I told them to turn from their evil ways –

MRS ALVING: *(At the window.)* Ahem.

MANDERS: I know, Engstrand – those brutes pushed you down the stairs. You've told me that before. Your injury does you credit.

ENGSTRAND: I don't want to boast about it, Pastor. But what I wanted to say is that when she confessed it all with eyes full of tears and a terrible gnashing of teeth, it broke my heart to hear it, I can tell you, your reverence.

MANDERS: Did it really, Engstrand? Well, what then?

ENGSTRAND: Well, I said, 'That American's roaming the high seas. And you, Joanna, have committed a sin and are a fallen woman. But here stands Jacob Engstrand, on two good legs' – that was just a way of speaking, of course, your reverence.

MANDERS: I understand. Go on.

ENGSTRAND: Well, sir, that's how I raised her up and made her my lawful wedded wife, so no one would know how bad she'd been with that foreigner.

MANDERS: Commendable. The only thing that can't be justified is taking the money.

ENGSTRAND: Me? Not a penny.

MANDERS: *(To MRS ALVING, with a questioning stare.)* But –

ENGSTRAND: Oh, aye – wait a bit – I remember now. Joanna did have a bob or two, as a matter of fact. But I didn't want anything to do with it. 'Fie,' I said, 'that's the wages of sin. This nasty gold' – banknotes, or whatever – 'let's chuck it back in the American's face'. But he'd vanished, across the stormy seas, your reverence.

MANDERS: Had he, my good man?

ENGSTRAND: He had. So Joanna and I decided the money should go towards the child's upbringing, and that's what happened. I can account for every penny.

MANDERS: Well, that changes everything.

ENGSTRAND: That's right, your reverence. And I think I've been an honourable father to Regina – as far as my strength allowed, of course – I'm mortal flesh, alas.

MANDERS: Come now, my dear Engstrand.

ENGSTRAND: I will say that I brought up the child well and was a loving husband to my poor Joanna, may she rest in peace, and kept a good house as the Bible says. But it never occurred to me to go to the Pastor and boast about it, just because I'd done one good deed in the world. No, when Jacob Engstrand does a good deed, he holds his tongue. Unfortunately, it doesn't happen often, as you know all too well. Which is why, whenever I visit your reverence, I never have anything but trouble and strife to talk about. Because, as I said – and I'll say it again – a conscience can be a messy thing.

MANDERS. Give me your hand, Jacob Engstrand.

ENGSTRAND: Oh, Pastor, I don't want –

MANDERS: No nonsense,

Shakes his hand.

There.

ENGSTRAND: And may I humbly beg your reverence's pardon –

MANDERS: You? On the contrary, it's for me to beg your pardon –

ENGSTRAND: Oh, Lord, sir, no.

MANDERS: And I do so with all my heart. Forgive me for having so misjudged you. And I assure you if I can do anything as a token of my goodwill towards you –

ENGSTRAND: Would you, sir?

MANDERS: With the greatest pleasure.

ENGSTRAND: As a matter of fact, sir, you might be able to do something right now. I'm thinking of using the few pennies I've put aside from my wages to open a home for sailors in town.

MRS ALVING: You?

ENGSTRAND: Aye, a refuge – like your orphanage. Many are the temptations that lie in wait for the poor sailor on shore. But in this home of mine he'll have a father's care.

MANDERS: What do you say to that, Mrs Alving?

ENGSTRAND: I haven't got much to put down, Heaven knows; but if I had a helping hand, well –

MANDERS: Quite so, let's talk about it soon. It's not an unattractive proposition. But now, I want you to go back to the orphanage and prepare everything nicely. And light the candles, so it's a bit festive. And then we'll have an edifying time together, my dear Engstrand, for I can see that you are in the right frame of mind.

ENGSTRAND: I think I am, to tell you the truth. So, goodbye, Mrs Alving, and thank you for everything. And take good care of Regina for me.

Wipes a tear from his eye.

Poor Joanna's wee child – it's odd, but she's become part of my life and tugs at my heart. Aye, that's how I feel.

Bows, and goes out.

MANDERS: Well, what do you think of him now, Mrs Alving? That was a very different explanation.

MRS ALVING: Yes, it was.

MANDERS: You see how careful we should be about condemning our fellow man. But what joy to discover that we were wrong. What do you think?

MRS ALVING: I think you're a baby, Pastor Manders, and always will be.

MENDERS: Me?

MRS ALVING: *(Laying her hands on his shoulders.)* And I'd like to throw my arms around you and give you a great big hug.

MANDERS: *(Drawing back hastily.)* Good lord. What an idea.

MRS ALVING: *(With a smile.)* Oh, you don't have to be afraid of me.

MANDERS: *(Standing by the table.)* You have such an extravagant way of putting things. I'll just gather these papers together and put them safely in my case.

Does so.

There. So, goodbye for now. Keep your eyes open when Osvald comes back. I'll come and see you later.

He takes his hat and goes out through the hall door. MRS ALVING sighs, glances out of the window, tidies one or two things up and turns to go into the dining-room. She stops in the doorway with a stifled cry.

MRS ALVING: Osvald, are you still in there?

OSVALD: *(From the dining-room.)* I'm just finishing my cigar.

MRS ALVING: I thought you'd gone out for a walk.

OSVALD: *(From within the room.)* In this weather?

A glass is heard clinking. MRS ALVING leaves the door open and sits down with her knitting on the sofa by the window.

Wasn't that Pastor Manders leaving just now?

MRS ALVING: Yes, he's gone down to the orphanage.

OSVALD: I see.

The clink of a bottle on a glass again.

MRS ALVING: *(Worried.)* Osvald, dear, you should be careful with that liqueur. It's very strong.

OSVALD: It keeps the damp out.

MRS ALVING: Wouldn't you rather come in here with me?

OSVALD: You know you don't like smoking in there.

MRS ALVING: You can smoke a cigar.

OSVALD: All right. Just one more drop. There.

Comes in, smoking a cigar, and shuts the door after him. A short silence.

Where's the Pastor?

MRS ALVING: I told you, he's gone over to the orphanage.

OSVALD: So you did.

MRS ALVING: You shouldn't sit so long at table, Osvald.

OSVALD: *(Holding his cigar behind his back.)* But it's so nice, mother dear.

Caresses her with one hand.

Think about it – to be home again, sitting at my mother's table, in my mother's dining-room, and enjoying her delicious meals.

MRS ALVING: My darling boy

OSVALD: *(a little impatiently, as he walks up and down smoking.)* What else is there for me to do? I can't work.

MRS ALVING: Can't work?

OSVALD: Not in this weather, without a glimpse of the sun.

Walks up and down the floor.

Not being able to work, it's –

MRS ALVING: Maybe it was a mistake to come home.

OSVALD: Mother, I had to.

MRS ALVING: Because I'd much rather sacrifice the pleasure of having you at home with me, than see you –

OSVALD: *(Standing still by the table.)* Tell me, mother – is it really such a pleasure to have me here?

MRS ALVING: How can you ask?

OSVALD: *(Crumpling up a newspaper.)* I thought it wouldn't matter if I was alive or dead.

MRS ALVING: How can you say that to your own mother, Osvald?

OSVALD: You've been perfectly happy without me.

MRS ALVING: Yes, I've lived without you – that's true.

A silence. The evening draws in. OSVALD paces up and down. He puts his cigar down.

OSVALD: *(Stopping beside MRS ALVING.)* Mother, may I sit beside you?

MRS ALVING: Of course, darling boy.

OSVALD: *(Sitting down.)* I have something to tell you, mother.

MRS ALVING: *(Anxiously.)* Alright.

OSVALD: *(Staring in front of him.)* Because I can't bear it any longer.

MRS ALVING: Bear what? What is it?

OSVALD: *(As before.)* I couldn't write about it, and since I've been home –

MRS ALVING: *(Catching him by the arm.)* Osvald, what is all this?

OSVALD: I tried to stop thinking about it – yesterday, today – to free myself of it. But I can't.

MRS ALVING: *(Getting up.)* Speak clearly, Osvald.

OSVALD: *(Drawing her down to her seat again.)* Sit still, and I'll try to tell you. I've complained a lot about being tired after the journey –

MRS ALVING: Well?

OSVALD: But that isn't the problem. This is no ordinary tiredness –

MRS ALVING: *(Trying to get up.)* You're not ill, Osvald, are you?

OSVALD: *(Pulling her down again.)* Be still, mother. Calm down. I'm not ill exactly – not in the usual sense.

Takes his head in his hands.

It's my spirit that's broken – it's destroyed – I'll never work again.

Buries his face in her lap and sobs.

MRS ALVING: *(Pale and trembling.)* Osvald, look at me. No, no, this isn't true.

OSVALD: *(Looking up with a distracted expression.)* I'll never work again. Never. It's a living death. Oh, mother, can you imagine anything so horrible?

MRS ALVING: My poor boy. How did this terrible thing happen?

OSVALD: *(Sitting up again.)* That's what I don't understand. I've not lived badly. Not at all. You mustn't think that, mother, I've never done that.

MRS ALVING: I'm sure, Osvald.

OSVALD: But this happens all the same, this terrible disaster.

MRS ALVING: It'll pass, darling boy. It's overwork, that's all. I promise.

OSVALD: *(Dully.)* I thought so too, at first. But it isn't.

MRS ALVING: Tell me everything.

OSVALD: I will.

MRS ALVING: When did you first notice anything?

OSVALD: It was just after I'd been here last time and had returned to Paris. I started getting these terrible headaches – mostly at the back, I think. It was as if an iron band was wrapped around my neck.

MRS ALVING: And then?

OSVALD: At first I thought it was just that problem I had when I was young.

MRS ALVING: Yes, yes.

OSVALD: But it wasn't, I soon realised. I couldn't paint any more. I'd start on some big new piece, but it was as if my talent had left me, as if my strength had gone. I couldn't focus, my head was swimming – everything went round and round. It was horrible. In the end, I saw a doctor – and he gave me the answer.

MRS ALVING: What do you mean?

OSVALD: He was one of the best doctors in Paris. He made me tell him how I felt, and asked dozens of questions which seemed completely irrelevant. I couldn't see what he was driving at –

MRS ALVING: Well?

OSVALD: Finally he said: 'You've had this canker from birth, you're worm-eaten' – 'vermoulu' as he put it...

MRS ALVING: *(Anxiously.)* What did he mean by that?

OSVALD: I didn't understand it, either, so I asked for an explanation. And then the old cynic said –

Clenches his fist.

Oh.

MRS ALVING: What did he say?

OSVALD: He said: 'The sins of the father are visited on the son.'

MRS ALVING: *(Getting up slowly.)* 'The sins of the father' –

OSVALD: I nearly punched him in the face.

MRS ALVING: *(Walking across the room.)* 'The sins of the father' –

OSVALD: *(Smiling sadly.)* Yes, imagine. So, of course, I told him that was ridiculous. But d'you think he listened, even then? No, he kept going on; and it was only when I showed him your letters and translated all the passages about father –

MRS ALVING: What then?

OSVALD: Well, of course, he had to admit that he was on the wrong track. And so I learned the truth – the terrible truth. That I should have avoided all those happy times I spent with my comrades. It was too much for me, you see. So, it's all my fault.

MRS ALVING: No, Osvald. Don't think like that –

OSVALD: There was no other explanation. And that's the worst thing about it. My whole life ruined – because of my own stupidity. Everything I wanted to do – I didn't dare think about it – I couldn't think about it. If only I could live my life over again – undo what's been done.

Throws himself face down on the sofa. MRS ALVING wrings her hands, and walks about silently struggling with herself.

OSVALD: *(Looks up after a while, raising himself on his elbows.)* If it had been something I'd inherited – something I couldn't help. But this. To have thrown away my happiness, my health, my whole life, so stupidly.

MRS ALVING: No, my darling boy, that's not possible.

Bending over him.

It's not as bad as you think.

OSVALD: Oh, you don't know –

Springs up.

And then to pass all this sorrow on to you. I've sometimes wished you didn't care about me so much.

MRS ALVING: Me, Osvald? My only son? The only thing I have in the world? The only person I love?

OSVALD: *(Taking hold of her hands and kissing them.)* Yes, yes, I know that, of course. When I'm here I know that's true. And that's one of the worst parts of it. But now you know, and let's not talk about it anymore. I can't stand thinking about it for long.

Walks across the room.

Let me have something to drink, mother.

MRS ALVING: To drink? What do you want to drink now?

OSVALD: Oh, anything. You must have some punch somewhere.

MRS ALVING: Yes, but Osvald, darling –

OSVALD: Don't, mother, please. I must have something to drown this misery.

Goes into the conservatory.

And it's so – gloomy in here.

MRS ALVING rings the bell.

And this endless rain. It can go on like this, week after week – for months. Never a ray of sunlight. I don't think I've seen the sun once since I've been back.

MRS ALVING: Osvald – you're thinking about leaving me again.

OSVALD: Hm –

Sighs deeply.

I'm not thinking about anything. I can't think about anything.

In a low voice.

But I probably won't.

REGINA: *(Coming from the dining-room.)* Did you ring, ma'am?

MRS ALVING: Yes, let's have a lamp in here.

REGINA: Straightaway, ma'am, it's already lit.

Goes out.

MRS ALVING: *(Going up to OSVALD.)* Osvald, don't hide anything from me.

OSVALD: I won't, mother.

Goes to the table.

I think I've told you a great deal.

REGINA brings the lamp in and puts it on the table.

MRS ALVING: Regina, you might bring us a half bottle of champagne.

REGINA: Yes, ma'am.

Goes out.

OSVALD: *(Taking hold of his mother's face.)* That's better, I knew my mother wouldn't let her son go thirsty.

MRS ALVING: My poor dear Osvald, how could I refuse you anything now?

OSVALD: *(Eagerly.)* Is that true, mother? Do you mean that?

MRS ALVING: Mean what?

OSVALD: That you couldn't refuse me anything?

MRS ALVING: My dear Osvald –

OSVALD: Sssh.

> *REGINA brings in a tray with a half bottle of champagne and two glasses, which she puts on the table.*

REGINA: Shall I open it?

OSVALD: No, thanks, I'll do it.

> *REGINA goes out.*

MRS ALVING: *(Sitting clown at the table.)* What did you mean, that I shouldn't refuse you?

OSVALD: *(Busy opening the bottle.)* First, let's have a drink – or two.

> *He pulls the cork, fills one glass and is about to fill the other.*

MRS ALVING: *(Holding her hand over the second glass.)* No, thanks – not for me.

OSVALD: For me then.

> *He empties his glass, refills it and empties it again; then sits at the table.*

MRS ALVING: *(Expectantly.)* Well?

OSVALD: *(Without looking at her.)* Tell me: I thought you and Manders looked strangely – subdued at dinner.

MRS ALVING: You noticed, did you?

OSVALD: Yes. Hm.

> *After a short pause.*

So, tell me – what do you think of Regina?

MRS ALVING: What do I think?

OSVALD: Yes, isn't she splendid?

MRS ALVING: Dear Osvald, you don't know her as well as I do –

OSVALD: So?

MRS ALVING: Regina lived at her home for too long, sadly. I should have taken her in earlier.

OSVALD: Yes, but isn't she splendid to look at, mother?

Fills his glass.

MRS ALVING: Regina has many serious flaws –

OSVALD: What does that matter?

Drinks.

MRS ALVING: I'm fond of her, all the same, and I feel responsible for her. I couldn't bear it if she came to any harm.

OSVALD: *(Jumping up.)* Mother, Regina is my only hope.

MRS ALVING: *(Getting up.)* What do you mean?

OSVALD: I can't suffer this agony alone.

MRS ALVING: Don't you have your mother to help you?

OSVALD: Yes, I thought I did, and that's why I came home. But it's no use, I can see, it's impossible. I can't live here.

MRS ALVING: Osvald.

OSVALD: I need another kind of life, mother, which is why I have to leave you. I don't want you watching me.

MRS ALVING: Oh, my poor unhappy boy. But, Osvald, so long as you're ill –

OSVALD: If it was just the illness, I'd probably stay, mother. You're my best friend in the world.

MRS ALVING: I am, Osvald, aren't I?

OSVALD: *(Walking restlessly about.)* But all this pain and regret – and fear. Oh – this terrible fear.

MRS ALVING: *(Following him.)* Fear? Of what? What do you mean?

OSVALD: Please don't. I don't know. I can't put it into words.

MRS ALVING crosses the room and rings the bell.

What do you want?

MRS ALVING: I want my boy to be happy, that's what I want. He mustn't worry all the time.

To REGINA, who has come to the door.

More champagne – a bottle.

OSVALD: Mother.

MRS ALVING: Do you think we country people don't know how to live?

OSVALD: Isn't she splendid? What a figure. The picture of health.

MRS ALVING: *(Sitting down at the table.)* Sit down, Osvald, and let's talk.

OSVALD: *(Sitting down.)* I'm sure you don't know, mother, but I've done Regina a wrong and I'm in her debt.

MRS ALVING: Really?

OSVALD: Just a little thoughtlessness – call it what you like. And quite innocent, by the way. The last time I was home –

MRS ALVING: Yes?

OSVALD: – she kept asking me about Paris, and I told her all sorts of things about my life there. And I remember saying one day: 'Would you like to go there yourself?'

MRS ALVING: Well?

OSVALD: I saw her blush, and she said: 'Very much.' 'All right,' I said, 'I'm sure that can be arranged' – or something like that.

MRS ALVING: And then?

OSVALD: Well, of course, I forgot all about it. But the day before yesterday when I asked her if she was happy that I was staying here for so long –

MRS ALVING: Well?

OSVALD: – she looked at me strangely, and said: 'But what about my trip to Paris?'

MRS ALVING: Her trip to Paris?

OSVALD: And then I found out that she'd taken the whole thing completely seriously, and had been thinking about me all the time, and had even started to learn French –

MRS ALVING: So that's why –

OSVALD: Oh mother – when I saw that beautiful, healthy young girl standing in front of me – I'd never really noticed her before – but there she was with her arms open as if she wanted to embrace me –

MRS ALVING: Osvald.

OSVALD: – and I realised that that's where my salvation lay, because she was so full of joy in life.

MRS ALVING: *(Starting back.)* Joy in life – ? Is there salvation in that?

REGINA: *(Coming in from the dining-room with a bottle of champagne.)* I'm sorry I took so long, but I had to go down to the cellar.

Puts the bottle on the table.

OSVALD: And bring another glass.

REGINA: *(Looking at him in astonishment.)* Madam's glass is there, Master Alving.

OSVALD: Yes, but get one for yourself, Regina.

REGINA starts, and gives a quick shy glance at MRS ALVING.

Well?

REGINA: *(In a low and hesitating voice.)* Is that alright, ma'am?

MRS ALVING: Fetch the glass, Regina.

REGINA goes into the dining-room.

OSVALD: *(Looking after her.)* Have you noticed the way she walks? – so firm, so confident.

MRS ALVING: Osvald, this is impossible.

OSVALD: It's decided. You must see that. There's no point trying to stop it.

REGINA comes in with a glass, which she keeps in her hand.

Sit down, Regina.

REGINA looks questioningly at MRS ALVING.

MRS ALVING: Sit down.

REGINA sits down on a chair near the dining-room door, still holding a glass.

Osvald, what was that you were saying about the joy in life?

OSVALD: Yes, mother, joy in life. You don't know much about that here. I never feel it here.

MRS ALVING: Not even when you're with me?

OSVALD: Not here. But you don't understand.

MRS ALVING: I think I do – now.

OSVALD: That – and the joy in work. They're the same thing really. But you can't know anything about that either.

MRS ALVING: Perhaps you're right there. Tell me more, Osvald.

OSVALD: Well, what I mean is that people here are taught to think that work is a curse and a punishment for their sins, and that life is wretched and the sooner it's over the better.

MRS ALVING: 'A vale of tears,' yes. And we make it like that.

OSVALD: But they'll have none of that over there. Nobody believes in things like that any more. There, just being

67

alive is a cause for happiness. Mother, have you noticed that everything I've painted has been about the joy in life? – always, always the joy in life. Light, sunshine and Sundays off – faces shining with happiness. That's why I'm afraid of staying here with you.

MRS ALVING: Afraid? What are you afraid of?

OSVALD: I'm afraid that everything good in me will turn ugly.

MRS ALVING: *(Looking steadily at him.)* Do you really think so?

OSVALD: I'm sure of it. Even if I lived here the same way that I do there – it wouldn't ever be the same.

MRS ALVING: *(Who has listened anxiously, gets up with a thoughtful expression and says.)* Now I see how it happened.

OSVALD: What do you see?

MRS ALVING: I see it, for the first time. And now I can speak.

OSVALD: *(Getting up.)* Mother, I don't understand.

REGINA: *(Who has got up also.)* I'd better go.

MRS ALVING: No, stay. Now I can speak. Now, my darling son, you shall know the whole truth. And then you can choose. Osvald. Regina.

OSVALD: Ssh – it's the Pastor.

MANDERS comes in by the hall door.

MANDERS: Well, friends, we've had a most edifying time down there.

OSVALD: So have we.

MANDERS: Engstrand must be helped with his sailors' hostel. And Regina will go with him.

REGINA: No, thank you, Pastor Manders.

MANDERS: *(Sees her for the first time.)* What, are you here? – with a glass in your hand.

REGINA: *(Putting down the glass hastily.)* Pardonnez moi –

OSVALD: Regina's going away with me, Pastor Manders.

MANDERS: Going away? With you?

OSVALD: Yes, as my wife – if she wants.

MANDERS: But, good heavens –

REGINA: It's not my fault, Pastor Manders.

OSVALD: Or else she'll stay here, if I do.

REGINA: *(Involuntarily.)* Here?

MANDERS: I'm appalled, Mrs Alving.

MRS ALVING: Neither of these things will happen, for now I can speak openly.

MANDERS: But you mustn't. No, no, don't.

MRS ALVING: I both can and will. And without destroying anyone's ideals.

OSVALD: Mother, what are you hiding from me?

REGINA: *(Listening.)* Madam, listen, what's that shouting?

Goes into the conservatory and looks out.

OSVALD: *(Going to the window on the left.)* What happening? Where's that light coming from?

REGINA: *(Calls out.)* The orphanage is on fire.

MRS ALVING: *(Going to the window.)* On fire?

MANDERS: On fire? Impossible. I was there a moment ago.

OSVALD: Where's my hat? Never mind. Father's orphanage –

Runs out through the garden door.

MRS ALVING: My shawl, Regina. The whole place is going up in flames.

MANDERS: How terrible. Mrs Alving, this fire is a judgment on this house of sin.

MRS ALVING: Yes, I'm sure. Come, Regina.

She and REGINA hurry out.

MANDERS: *(Clasping his hands.)* And no insurance.

Follows them out.

ACT THREE

All the doors are open. The lamp is still burning on the table. It's dark outside, except for a faint glow visible through the windows at the back.

MRS ALVING, with a large shawl over her head, is standing in the conservatory, looking out. REGINA, also in a shawl, is standing just behind her.

MRS ALVING: It's all burnt down – to the ground.

REGINA: There's still fire in the cellar.

MRS ALVING: Why doesn't Osvald come back? There's nothing left to save.

REGINA: Perhaps I should take him his hat?

MRS ALVING: He hasn't got his hat?

REGINA: *(Pointing to the hall.)* No, look, it's hanging up in there.

MRS ALVING: Leave it. He's got to come back soon. I'll go and find him.

Goes out the garden door. MANDERS comes in from the hall.

MANDERS: Isn't Mrs Alving here?

REGINA: She's just gone down into the garden.

MANDERS: This has been the worst night of my life.

REGINA: A real disaster, isn't it, sir?

MANDERS: Don't speak of it. I hardly dare think about it.

REGINA: But how could it have happened, Pastor?

MANDERS: Don't ask, Miss Engstrand. How should I know?
  Are you suggesting – ? It's bad enough that your father –

REGINA: What's he done?

MANDERS: He's driving me mad.

ENGSTRAND: *(Coming in from the hall.)* Pastor Manders –

MANDERS: *(Turning round with a start.)* Are you still chasing after me?

ENGSTRAND: Aye, God help me, I had to – But, Lord, what a terrible business, your reverence.

MANDERS: *(Walking up and down.)* Yes, yes, I'm afraid so.

REGINA: What do you mean?

ENGSTRAND: It was because of our little prayer-meeting, wasn't it?

Aside, to REGINA.

We've got him now, my girl.

Aloud.

And to think it's all my fault that Pastor Manders was responsible for it.

MANDERS: But I assure you, Engstrand –

ENGSTRAND: You were the only one mucking around with candles, sir.

MANDERS: *(Standing still.)* So you say. But I have no memory of holding one.

ENGSTRAND: But, sir, I distinctly saw you snuff out a candle with your fingers and drop the wick into the wood shavings.

MANDERS: You saw me do that?

ENGSTRAND: Clear as daylight.

MANDERS: I just don't understand. I never snuff out candles with my fingers.

ENGSTRAND: Ay, it looked awfully careless, sir. But is it really that bad?

MANDERS: *(Pacing up and down.)* Oh, don't ask.

ENGSTRAND: *(Following him about.)* And your reverence hadn't insured it, either, had you?

MANDERS: No – as I told you.

ENGSTRAND: Hadn't insured it. And then went and set light to the whole place? Good Lord, that's a real disaster.

MANDERS: *(Wiping the perspiration from his forehead.)* You can say that again, Engstrand.

ENGSTRAND: And to a charitable institution, that would have helped the whole region, as they say. The newspapers won't be kind, I'm afraid.

MANDERS: That's what I keep thinking. It's almost the worst part of the whole thing. The personal attacks – oh, it's terrible.

MRS ALVING: *(Coming in from the garden.)* I can't get him away from the fire.

MANDERS: Ah, there you are, Mrs Alving.

MRS ALVING: Well, you won't have to make your speech now, Pastor Manders.

MANDERS: Oh, I'd happily have –

MRS ALVING: *(In a dull voice.)* Just as well. The orphanage would never have come to any good.

MANDERS: Don't you think so?

MRS ALVING: Do you?

MANDERS: It was terribly bad luck all the same.

MRS ALVING: Well, let's just treat it as a business matter, alright? Are you waiting for the Pastor, Engstrand?

ENGSTRAND: *(At the hall door.)* I am, yes.

MRS ALVING: Well, do sit down for a moment.

ENGSTRAND: Thank you, I'd rather stand.

MRS ALVING: *(To MANDERS.)* You're taking the steamer back to town, I presume?

MANDERS: Yes, it sails in an hour –

MRS ALVING: Would you take all these documents with you? I don't want to hear another word on the matter. I've other things to think about now.

MANDERS: Mrs Alving –

MRS ALVING: I'll send you power of attorney to deal with it all, however you like.

MANDERS: Gladly. I'm afraid the original terms of the bequest will have to be changed.

MRS ALVING: Of course.

MANDERS: For now, I suggest you turn 'Sunlit Bay' over to the parish. The land isn't without value; it'll always have its uses. As for the interest in the bank, well, perhaps I could use it for something that benefits the town.

MRS ALVING: Whatever you like. It means nothing to me now.

ENGSTRAND: Don't forget my sailors' hostel, Pastor.

MANDERS: That's one possibility. We'll have to judge it on its merits.

ENGSTRAND: *(Aside.)* Oh, to hell with that – pardon me.

MANDERS: *(Sighing.)* And, unfortunately, I don't know how much longer I'll be dealing with such matters – public opinion may force me to step down. It all depends on the investigations into the fire.

MRS ALVING: What did you say?

MANDERS: And we can't predict the outcome.

ENGSTRAND: *(Going nearer to him.)* Oh yes, we can. Because here stands Jacob Engstrand.

MANDERS: Quite so, but –

ENGSTRAND: *(Lowering his voice.)* And Jacob Engstrand isn't the sort of man to desert a benefactor in his hour of need, as the saying goes.

MANDERS: Yes, my dear fellow, but how – ?

ENGSTRAND: *(with full Engstrand* is like a guardian angel, your reverence.

MANDERS: No, no, I couldn't possibly accept that.

ENGSTRAND: But that's how it'll be. I know a man who took the blame for another man before.

MANDERS: Oh, Jacob, Jacob.

Grasps his hand.

You're one in a thousand. You'll get help for your hostel, I can promise you that.

ENGSTRAND tries to thank him, but is prevented by emotion.

MANDERS: *(Slinging his bag over his shoulder.)* Now let's be off. We'll go together.

ENGSTRAND: *(By the dining-room door, says aside to REGINA.)* Why don't you come home with me, my girl? You'd be snug as a bug in a rug.

REGINA: *(Tossing her head.)* Merçi.

She goes out into the hall and brings MANDERS' travelling clothes.

MANDERS: Live well, Mrs Alving. And may law and order return to this house soon.

MRS ALVING: Farewell, Manders.

She goes into the conservatory and sees OSVALD coming in by the garden door.

ENGSTRAND: *(As he and REGINA help MANDERS on with his coat.)* Farewell, my child. And if you're ever in any trouble, you know where to find Jacob Engstrand.

Lowering his voice.

Little Harbour Street, alright?

To MRS ALVING and OSVALD.

And my sailors hostel will be called 'The Court Chamberlain Alving Home'. And, if I can run it the way I want to, I think it'll deserve that noble gentleman's name.

MANDERS: *(At the door.)* Ahem. Come along then, my dear Engstrand. Goodbye, goodbye.

He and ENGSTRAND go out by the hall door.

OSVALD: *(Going to the table.)* What was he talking about?

MRS ALVING: Oh, some sort of hostel that he and Pastor Manders want to open.

OSVALD: It'll burn down just like this one.

MRS ALVING: What makes you say that?

OSVALD: Everything will burn. Nothing will be left to remind us of father. I'm being burnt, too.

REGINA looks at him in alarm.

MRS ALVING: Osvald. You shouldn't have stayed down there so long, my poor boy.

OSVALD: *(Sitting down at the table.)* I think you might be right.

MRS ALVING: Let me dry your face, Osvald, you're soaking.

Dries his face with her handkerchief.

OSVALD: *(Looking straight before him, with no expression in his eyes.)* Thank you, mother.

MRS ALVING: Aren't you tired, Osvald? Don't you want to sleep?

OSVALD: *(Uneasily.)* Sleep? No – I never sleep, I just pretend.

Gloomily.

That'll come soon enough.

MRS ALVING: *(Looking at him anxiously.)* You really are ill, darling boy.

REGINA: *(Intently.)* Is Master Alving ill?

OSVALD: *(Impatiently.)* And shut all the doors. This fear –

MRS ALVING: Shut them, Regina.

> *REGINA shuts the doors and stands by the hall door. MRS ALVING takes off her shawl; REGINA does the same. MRS ALVING draws up a chair beside OSVALD and sits down.*

There. I'll sit down beside you –

OSVALD: Yes, do. And Regina must stay; she must be with me always. You'll give me a helping hand, Regina, won't you?

REGINA: I don't understand –

MRS ALVING: A helping hand?

OSVALD: Yes – when it's needed.

MRS ALVING: Osvald, don't you have your mother to give you a helping hand?

OSVALD: You?

> *Smiles.*

No, mother, you could never give me the helping hand I need.

> *Laughs grimly.*

You? Ha, ha.

> *Looks seriously at her.*

Even though you have the most right to do so.

> *Suddenly angry, to REGINA.*

Why can't you be freer with me? Why don't you call me Osvald?

REGINA: *(Quietly.)* I don't think Ma'am would like it.

MRS ALVING: You'll soon have the right to do so. Come and sit down here with us.

REGINA sits quietly and hesitatingly on the other side of the table.

And now, my poor tortured boy, I'm going to take a weight off your mind –

OSVALD: Are you, mother?

MRS ALVING: – all that guilt and regret.

OSVALD: And you think you can do that?

MRS ALVING: I can now, Osvald. You were talking earlier about joy in life, and what you said has shed light on everything in my life.

OSVALD: *(Shaking his head.)* I don't understand.

MRS ALVING: You should have known your father when he was young. He was full of joy in life, I can tell you.

OSVALD: Yes, I know.

MRS ALVING: It made me feel like Sunday weather just looking at him, full of such tremendous life and energy.

OSVALD: So what happened?

MRS ALVING: Well, this boy, so full of joy in life – he was just a boy, back then – well, he had to live in a small town with no joy, just diversions. He had to live a pointless life out here, as a government official. He had no real work, just routine. And not a single friend who could appreciate joy in life; just layabouts and drunks...

OSVALD: Mother –

MRS ALVING: And so the inevitable happened.

OSVALD: What inevitable?

MRS ALVING: You said earlier what you'd turn into if you stayed at home.

OSVALD: Do you mean that father – ?

MRS ALVING: Your poor father never found an outlet for that great joy in life inside him. And I didn't bring much, either.

OSVALD: You didn't?

MRS ALVING: I'd been taught duty, and all the things I believed in for so long. Everything came down to duty – my duty, his duty and – I'm afraid I made your poor father's home unbearable, Osvald.

OSVALD: Why didn't you say that in your letters?

MRS ALVING: I didn't see it as something I could tell his son.

OSVALD: How did you see it, then?

MRS ALVING: I just saw that your father was ruined even before you were born.

OSVALD: *(Quietly.)* Oh –

He gets up and goes to the window.

MRS ALVING: And then I thought about just one thing, day and night – that Regina belonged in this house – as much as my own son.

OSVALD: *(Turns suddenly.)* Regina – ?

REGINA: *(Gets up and asks quietly.)* Me – ?

MRS ALVING: Yes, so now you know, both of you.

OSVALD: Regina.

REGINA: *(To herself.)* So my mother was one of them, was she?

MRS ALVING: Your mother had many great qualities, Regina.

REGINA: Yes, but she was one of them, all the same. I guessed myself sometimes, but – Well, Mrs Alving, do I have your permission to leave now?

MRS ALVING: Do you really want to, Regina?

REGINA: Yes, I do.

MRS ALVING: Of course, you're free to do as you like, but –

OSVALD: *(Going up to REGINA.)* Leave? But this is your home.

REGINA: Merçi, Master Alving – oh, I suppose I can call you Osvald now, but not the way I'd hoped.

MRS ALVING: Regina, I've not been honest with you –

REGINA: No, you haven't. If I'd known that Osvald was ill – And now there can't be anything serious between us – No, I can't stay here, wearing myself out looking after sick people.

OSVALD: Not even a man who's so close to you?

REGINA: Not really. A poor girl must use her looks, or she'll find herself on the shelf. And I've got the joy in life in me too, Mrs Alving.

MRS ALVING: Yes, unfortunately. But don't throw yourself away, Regina.

REGINA: What will be, will be. If Osvald takes after his father, I suppose I take after my mother – But let me ask you, Mrs Alving, does Pastor Manders know this?

MRS ALVING: He knows everything.

REGINA: *(Putting on her shawl.)* Oh, well, the best thing I can do is catch the steamer as soon as I can. Pastor Manders is such a gentleman, he'll do right by me, and I have as much right to that money as – that awful carpenter.

MRS ALVING: You deserve it, Regina, really.

REGINA: *(Fixed on her.)* You should have brought me up as the daughter of a gentleman. It would have been more appropriate.

Tosses her head.

But what the hell – it doesn't matter.

With a bitter glance at the unopened bottle.

I'll be drinking champagne with the gentry one day, you'll see.

MRS ALVING: If you ever need a home, Regina, come to me.

REGINA: No, thank you, Mrs Alving. The Pastor will look after me. And if things don't work out, well, I know a place where I'll be wanted.

MRS ALVING: Where's that?

REGINA: 'The Court Chamberlain Alving Home.'

MRS ALVING: Regina – I can see it – you're going to your ruin.

REGINA: Pah – adieu.

She curtseys and goes out through the hall.

OSVALD: *(Standing by the window, looking out.)* Has she gone?

MRS ALVING: Yes.

OSVALD: *(Muttering to himself.)* It's all wrong, this.

MRS ALVING: *(Goes up to him behind and puts her hands on his shoulders.)* Osvald, my darling boy – has this come as a terrible shock?

OSVALD: *(Turning his face towards her.)* All this about my father, you mean?

MRS ALVING: Yes, your unhappy father. I'm afraid it's been too much for you.

OSVALD: What makes you say that? Of course, it was a big shock, but it doesn't affect me all that much.

MRS ALVING: *(Drawing back her hands.)* Doesn't affect you? – that your father's life was so unhappy?

OSVALD: Of course, I feel sorry for him, as I would for anyone, but –

MRS ALVING: Is that all? For your own father.

OSVALD: *(Impatiently.)* Oh, yes, father, father. I never knew anything about my father. All I remember is that he once made me sick.

MRS ALVING: That's terrible. Shouldn't a son love his father, whatever happens?

OSVALD: When the son has nothing to thank his father for? When he's never known him? Do you still believe in that old superstition, when you're so enlightened in other ways?

MRS ALVING: Superstition?

OSVALD: Yes, surely you can see that, mother. It's one of those ideas that goes around, but

MRS ALVING: *(Shaken.)* Ghosts.

OSVALD: *(Walking across the room.)* Yes, you could call them ghosts.

MRS ALVING: *(With feeling.)* So, Osvald, you don't love me either.

OSVALD: At least I know you –

MRS ALVING: Yes, but is that all?

OSVALD: And I know how fond you are of me, and I'm grateful to you for that. Besides, you can be helpful to me, now I'm ill.

MRS ALVING: I can, can't I? I could almost bless the illness which brought you home. I know you're not mine yet – and I must win you back.

OSVALD: *(Impatiently.)* Yes, yes, but that's just talk. Remember, I'm a sick man, mother. I can't think about anyone else. I've enough to do, just thinking about myself.

MRS ALVING: *(Gently.)* I'll be very good and patient.

OSVALD: And cheerful too, mother.

MRS ALVING: Yes, darling boy, you're right.

Goes up to him.

So, Osvald, tell me, have I taken away your feelings of guilt and regret?

OSVALD: Yes, you have. But who'll take away the fear?

MRS ALVING: The fear?

OSVALD: *(Crossing the room.)* Regina would have done it.

MRS ALVING: I don't understand. What is this fear? – and what's Regina got to do with it?

OSVALD: Is it very late, mother?

MRS ALVING: It's early morning.

Looks out through the conservatory windows.

The dawn's breaking on the mountains. And it's going to be a clear day, Osvald. Soon you'll be able to see the sun.

OSVALD: I'm glad. So there might be something for me to live for after all –

MRS ALVING: I hope so.

OSVALD: Even if I can't work –

MRS ALVING: Oh, you'll be able to work again soon. Now you don't have all those painful thoughts.

OSVALD: Yes, it's good you've been able to rid me of those. If I could just deal with this last thing –

Sits down on the couch.

Mother, we're going to talk now.

MRS ALVING: Yes.

Pushes an armchair near to the couch and sits beside him.

OSVALD: The sun's rising – and then you'll know. And I won't feel fear any longer.

MRS ALVING: What will I know?

OSVALD: *(Without listening to her.)* Mother, didn't you say earlier that there was nothing in the world you wouldn't do for me if I asked?

MRS ALVING: Yes, I did.

OSVALD: And will you keep your word, mother?

MRS ALVING: You can rely on that, my darling boy. I've nothing else to live for, just you.

OSVALD: Alright, I'll tell you – Listen, mother, you're very willful, I know. But I want you to sit quietly and listen.

MRS ALVING: But what is this terrible thing – ?

OSVALD: You mustn't scream. D'you hear? We're going to sit quietly and talk it over. Do you promise me that, mother?

MRS ALVING: Yes, yes, I promise – just tell me what it is.

OSVALD: Well, then, the fact is this tiredness of mine – my not being able to concentrate – that's not the real illness –

MRS ALVING: What is it then?

OSVALD: The illness is hereditary. It's –

He points to his forehead and speaks very quietly

– here.

MRS ALVING: *(Almost speechless.)* Osvald. No, no.

OSVALD: Don't scream, I can't bear it. Oh yes, it's in here, waiting. And it could break out any time, at any moment.

MRS ALVING: How horrible –

OSVALD: Please be calm. That's the state I'm in –

MRS ALVING: *(Springing up.)* It's not true, Osvald. It's impossible. It can't be.

OSVALD: I had one attack when I was away. It passed off quickly. But when they told me what it was, this terrible fear took hold of me. And then I came home to you as quickly as I could.

MRS ALVING: So that was the fear, then –

OSVALD: Yes, because it really is so horrible, you see. If it had been an ordinary illness – I'm not afraid of dying, though, of course, I'd like to live as long as I can.

MRS ALVING: Yes, Osvald, you must.

OSVALD: But this is unbearable. To be a child again, a baby –
to have to be fed, to have to be – Oh, it's indescribable.

MRS ALVING: A child has his mother to look after him.

OSVALD: *(Jumping up.)* No, no, that's exactly what I don't
want. I can't bear the idea of living like that for years –
getting old and grey. And you might die before I did.

Sits down in MRS ALVING's chair.

Because it isn't necessarily fatal, the doctor said. He called
it a 'softening of the brain' – something like that.

Smiles mournfully.

I think that sounds lovely. It makes me think of cherry red
velvet curtains – something soft to stroke.

MRS ALVING: *(With a scream.)* Osvald.

OSVALD: *(Jumps up and walks about the room.)* And now you've
taken Regina away from me. If only I had her, she'd have
given me a helping hand, I know.

MRS ALVING: *(Going up to him.)* Darling boy, what do you
mean? Is there anything in the world I wouldn't give you?

OSVALD: When I recovered from that attack in Paris, the
doctor said that when it recurred – and it will recur –
there'd be no more hope.

MRS ALVING: The heartless –

OSVALD: I made him tell me. I said I had arrangements to
make –

Smiles cunningly.

And I did.

Takes a small box from his inside pocket.

Mother, d'you see this?

MRS ALVING: What is it?

OSVALD: Morphine.

MRS ALVING: *(Looking at him in shock.)* Osvald – my boy.

OSVALD: I've got twelve tablets, saved up –

MRS ALVING: *(Snatching at it.)* Give me the box, Osvald.

OSVALD: Not yet, mother.

Puts it back in his pocket.

MRS ALVING: I'll never get over this.

OSVALD: You must get over it. If Regina was here, I'd have told her everything – and asked her for a final helping hand. She'd have helped me, I'm sure.

MRS ALVING: No.

OSVALD: If this terrible thing struck me down and she saw me lying there like a helpless baby, past help, past hope – past saving –

MRS ALVING: Regina would never have done it.

OSVALD: She would. Regina's so light-hearted. And she'd have got bored of looking after an invalid like me.

MRS ALVING: Then thank God Regina isn't here.

OSVALD: Now *you'll* have to give me that helping hand, mother.

MRS ALVING: *(With a loud scream.)* Me?

OSVALD: Who has the better right?

MRS ALVING: Your own mother?

OSVALD: That's why.

MRS ALVING: Me, who gave you life?

OSVALD: I never asked you for life. And what sort of a life has it been? I don't want it. Take it back.

MRS ALVING: Help. Help.

Runs into the hall.

OSVALD: *(Following her.)* Don't leave me. Where are you going?

MRS ALVING: *(In the hall.)* To get the doctor, Osvald. Let me go.

OSVALD: *(Going into the hall.)* You're not going to go. And no one's coming in either.

Turns the key in the lock.

MRS ALVING: *(Coming in again.)* Osvald, Osvald – my child.

OSVALD: *(Following her.)* Do you have a mother's heart – and you can bear me suffering like this?

MRS ALVING: *(Controlling herself, after a moment's silence.)* Here's my hand on it.

OSVALD: Will you – ?

MRS ALVING: If necessary. But it won't be necessary. No, no, it won't. It won't.

OSVALD: Let's hope not. And let's live together as long as we can. Thank you, mother.

He sits in the armchair, which MRS ALVING has moved beside the sofa. Day is breaking but the lamp is still burning on the table.

MRS ALVING: *(Approaches him cautiously.)* Do you feel calmer now?

OSVALD: Yes.

MRS ALVING: *(Bending over him.)* It's all just a figment of your imagination, Osvald. That's all. It's all been so difficult for you. But now you can rest, at home with your mother, my darling boy. You can have anything you want, just like when you were a child – There, now. The attack's passed. You see? I knew it would – And look, Osvald, it's going to be a beautiful day. Brilliant sunshine. You'll be able to see your home properly.

She goes to the table and puts out the lamp. It's sunrise. The glaciers and peaks in the distance are bathed in morning light.

OSVALD: *(Who has been sitting motionless in the armchair, with his back to the landscape outside, suddenly says.)* Mother, give me the sun.

MRS ALVING: *(Standing at the table, and looking at him with surprise.)* What did you say?

OSVALD: *(Repeats in a dull, toneless voice.)* The sun. The sun.

MRS ALVING: *(Going up to him.)* Osvald, what's the matter?

OSVALD seems to shrink in the chair. All his muscles relax, his face loses its expression, and his eyes stare vacantly. MRS ALVING is trembling with fear.

What is it?

Screams.

Osvald. What's the matter with you?

She kneels beside him and shakes him.

Osvald. Osvald. Look at me. Don't you recognise me.

OSVALD: *(Expressionless, as before.)* The sun – the sun.

MRS ALVING: *(Jumps up despairingly, tears at her hair and screams.)* I can't bear it.

Whispers as if paralysed.

I can't bear it... No, never.

Suddenly.

Where did he put them?

Passes her hand quickly over his coat.

Here.

Draws back a little and cries out:

No, no, no. – Yes. – no, no.

She stands a few steps from him, her hands in her hair, and stares at him in terror.

OSVALD: *(Sitting motionless, as before.)* The sun – the sun.

WWW.OBERONBOOKS.COM

Follow us on www.twitter.com/@oberonbooks
& www.facebook.com/OberonBooksLondon

Printed in the USA
CPSIA information can be obtained
at www.ICGtesting.com
LVHW011516181023
761467LV00005B/609

9 781783 190522